C000171763

Atlantis

The Origins Of Ancient Civilizations And Mystery

(New Evidence Of A Previous Technological Civilization)

David Gill

Published By **Jordan Levy**

David Gill

All Rights Reserved

*Atlantis: The Origins Of Ancient Civilizations
And Mystery (New Evidence Of A Previous
Technological Civilization)*

ISBN   978-1-7780579-5-3

Legal & Disclaimer

The information contained in this ebook is not designed to replace or take the place of any form of medicine or professional medical advice. The information in this ebook has been provided for educational & entertainment purposes only.

The information contained in this book has been compiled from sources deemed reliable, and it is accurate to the best of the Author's knowledge; however, the Author cannot guarantee its accuracy and validity and cannot be held liable for any errors or omissions. Changes are periodically made to this book. You must consult your doctor or get professional medical advice before using any of the suggested remedies, techniques, or information in this book.

Upon using the information contained in this book, you agree to hold harmless the Author from and against any damages, costs, and expenses, including any legal fees potentially resulting from the application of any of the

Table of contents

Introduction

A map from the 19th century that speculates about the size of Atlantis empire.

Atlantis

"And it was the Island of Atalantes that was larger that Africa and Asia and Asia, as Plato mentions in Timaeus In a single night and day, was swept by the sea as a result of an incredible earthquake and flood, and then abruptly vanished, becoming a sea, in fact, un-navigable however, it was filled with eddies and gulfs." first century CE Philosopher Philo"

The tale of Atlantis has captured the imaginations and the hearts of scientists, historians writers, artists, and scientists for centuries, yet it continues to amaze anyone when they learn that the sole evidence of literary origin available is one 4th century BCE writer. It was the Athenian philosopher Plato is well-known for his dialogues where his Socratic Method was invented, was the first person to refer to that mysterious planet of Atlantis. In his writings Timaeus and Critias, Plato describes the beginning of the tale of

Atlantis however, the Critias one, in which the more lengthy and more detailed description occurs, was never completed, and as such it has been a mystery germ of millennia of thought.

Within Timaeus, Plato envisions for the first time a godlike craftsman, or Demiurge (demiourgos 28a) who organizes an orderly, rational and teleologically functional universe. The creation process is directed by Demiurge's mind (nous) and is constructed according to mathematical rules. But, even Demiurge is limited by the fact that he is a the necessity of creating the universe. He can construct the universe in the best way as he can however, he cannot make it better. The prose and allegorical reference to the single god certainly encapsulated the medieval mindset by it's Latin interpretation of Calcidius (c. 321 C.E.) and for many centuries in time during the Middle Ages, Timaeus was the only Platonic dialogue that was available to those who had an interest in natural philosophy. it was lauded accordingly.

But, Timaeus is best remembered in the present for his description of Atlantis that Plato discusses in the dialogue Critias. In essence the text that Plato described of Atlantis contains all the components of a good Hollywood narrative, and the accuracy of an expert mapmaker. According to the legend that The god of the ocean Poseidon was granted an island called Atlantis (larger in size than Libya and Asia according to Plato) situated within the Pillars of Heracles. (This may be just as distant away from Greece than Gibraltar). The 10 sons of Poseidon, that were princes controlled the gorgeous island. It was fertile and abundant with resources, supplying everything that a paradise needs. However, Atlantis was not solely an uncultivated Garden of Eden. Fortifications roads, palaces, roads, and even constructions created this island a wealthy as well constructed city.

Plato is believed to have enjoyed providing detailed descriptions of the city's architectural features, which were designed to attract future explorers however, Renaissance authors Thomas More and Francis Bacon who wrote their novels Utopia (1516) in addition to New Atlantis (1627), were more interested in the next section of dialogue. In the Phaedrus-like moral and mortal journey from heaven towards earth people of Atlantis were able to take part within the spirit of God and abide by the rules. But when they fell short of their divine nature and ascended from the moral apex and fell into the human nature, the human spirit at work. Zeus determined to punish them. Atlantis is now sunk by earthquakes which has resulted in a wall of impervious mud, which blocks those sailing from the shores of Atlantis towards the ocean to the west from continuing further. Many films and novels starting with Journey to the Center of the Earth (1959) to in the latest adaptation of Scratlantis in Ice Age: Continental Drift (2012) which aims to return Plato's dream on the top of the world.

The character who is the title of Critias during the dialogues is seen throughout both works as one of the Socrates's friends. He is the one who tells the tale of Atlantis that he says is the same one that was told to Solon the Athenian politician Solon (638-558 BCE) by the wise priest of Egypt. In this version the two texts have been combined with direct quotes from both to provide an overall, more complete version of the Atlantian source. The descriptions of the society the geography, its society, and eventually decline are essential to comprehend how the later scholars came consider Atlantis as well as how they came to the different conclusions that continue to puzzle people to today.

Solon was believed to have been given the story of Atlantis -- a vast continent located beyond that of "Pillars of Hercules/Hercules" that today are called Gibraltar. Strait of Gibraltar -- while on his travels. it could be beneficial to know a bit more about the person who received the legend. Solon became the Archon (i.e. "Chief Magistrate") of Athens in the year 594-593 BCE and was later referred to as the 'founder of Democracy'. 1. A small portion of the work of this famous poet and politician composed has survived the epochs and the fragments that remain are not of the best quality and are not consistent in portraying his image as a hero of reformation in Athens. One particular fragment can be revealing of this almost legendary character. "This is what I've accomplished, using the power of the Law and the use of both justice and force. I've accomplished it until the very end in the way I said I would. I have outlined rulesthat are the same for the wicked as well as the righteous, granting justice to everyone. If another person had been in a position to follow this rule by a fool or selfish man, he may not have stifled the crowd. Because if I had been a slave to what the people in revolt wanted and what other side wanted and the city would be a widowed city with a lot of men. So, using all my might I fought on each side as a dog that was surrounded by wolves."[22

After he fought for the social justice reforms in Athens, Solon left the city for ten years. He went to different countries to study their past and their social structures. The reasoning behind this was logical as if he didn't live at Athens there was no way to make him, as Archon was able to do, to abolish the reforms. However, when he returned there was such a degraded atmosphere within the town that Archon was according to legend, prevented from writing the account of Atlantis his own. Plato says of his character as"not just the most intelligent of men however, in the realm of poetry, among all poets he was the noblest,"[3 and the possibility that he, like a mythological character is the main character in the story of a nearly perfect society from the past is significant in the true sense. The mystery and alleged historical significance of Solon is similar to the mystery of Atlantis however It was Atlantis that would win minds and hearts and inspire the same passion as other for generations to follow.

Chapter 1: The Story Of Atlantis

In the lush Nile Delta, where the trading vessels drift along the tributaries as if they were jetsam from their cities of origin There is Sais, the capital city. Sais. Much like Athens the city was founded by Athena in the beginning of the Age of the Gods, but in Sais she is referred to by her old Egyptian names, Neith as well as Isis. It was in Sais that the Great Amasis the King of Philhellene decided to establish his residence royal and it was also at the temple of the goddess of the past that Solon first learned of the connections between his home and theirs.

The mystic writings found on the temple's wall, as well as the wisdom spoken by priests led to Solon desire to build a rapport with his host So he informed them about the oldest tale he could remember: the story of Deucalion the last good man from the hubristic Bronze Age, who, along with his wife Pyrrha endured the terrible flood that was sparked by Zeus in his fury. It was the obligation of this couple to rebuild the earth after the waters were slowed down. Solon was reminiscing about the stories of the

8

Deucalion and Pyrrrha's descendants, when the priest of old interrupted him and said, "O Solon, Solon You Greeks have always been children. There's nothing like an older Greek." When hearing this , he asked, "What mean you by this statement?" And the priest responded, "You are young in soul, each and every one of you. You do not hold any belief that is old and originated from traditions, nor a single scientific discipline that becomes obsolete as you age."[55

An old bust depicting Solon

Solon was stunned however, the priest proved his point by giving a brief speech in which he listed the stories that the Greeks were familiar with and believed in for centuries, including the tale that tells of Phaethon, Helios the Sun's boy, who had tied his father's chariot and in not being so strong or as godlike as he was, let the reins slip away from him, causing the sun to deviate away from its path, and then draw closer to the soil, burning crops and cities as it travelled. The story, as the priest claimed was not a literary fanciful tale. The races that are now lost to the passage of time and story races, races who had attempted to understand the devastating fire that affected these races, wrote their tale of Phaethon several generations back.

Priest explained celestial bodies naturally and frequently were drawn closer to the earth by themselves. This is why the earth was afflicted with scorching droughts as well as destructive floods like the ones Deucalion and Pyrrha observed in their vessel. In the same way, while hundreds of Greeks were swept away by the floods , and were starving during droughts, the Egyptians weren't affected. Their water didn't fall out of the sky and resurfaced out of the vital Nile as fertile crop. The fertile Delta is already in the desert, did not have to worry about droughts. In fact, in the past it was able to draw from its mystical source during times of great necessity. The priest stretched his arms and showed Solon the scrolls that were affixed to around the temple's walls. "Hence it is because of this reason, what's there preserved is thought to be the oldest but the reality is that wherever there isn't a lot of temperature or cold to stop it, there will always be a human race, today more and now less. In the event that an event was to occur that was significant or great, or even arousing regardless of whether it was in your country , ours, or even in a different area that we are aware of through reports, all of these incidents are documented from ancient times and preserved in our temples, however, your people and other people are also constantly being re-equipped with the latest technology, including letters and kinds of arts that civilized States require. When after the normal interval of time, similar to an epidemic the flood from heaven descends on your people, it removes none of you except the unliterate and uncultured, causing you are as young as ever and have no idea of what happened during the past, whether either in this region or your own."[66

The priest put his hand on the shoulder of Solon. He explained to Solon that learning the hundreds of generations Solon had recollected was an incredible feat for the human brain however Solon's Egyptians maintained records that made Solon's solemn story appear to be an unimportant children's tale. Solon informed him that Athens as well as all Greeks were closer with the Egyptians than they thought that they were related to each other. The flood that Solon had known of was the first of many but generations that followed were numerous. Every time, the

Greeks needed to start over building their homes and replant their farm however, they had lost the history of their grandparents along with the fact that they, as nation were fresh as ever. The youthfulness of their cultural heritage was renewed with each disaster they faced and they never realized that the Greeks particularly had ties to the oldest civilization on the coasts of the Mediterranean. "For it is true that at one period, Solon, before the most devastating destruction caused by flood, the area that is today known as the Athenian State was one of the most courageous in battle and the most well-organized in other aspects. It was said to have was home to the most beautiful works of art as well as the most noble polity of any nation that we've seen or heard tell."[77

The priest took out a scroll , and then unfurled the scroll before Solon. He explained to the Greek that this was one of the genealogies that the Egyptians had and, when taken together they proved how their people -- also known as the "People of Athena" -lived in the lush land for over 8000 years. Genealogies weren't just list of names. They were a collection of stories about men and gods as well as the cycle in the world.

The priest was fond of Solon. He believed that he was a moral man who sought out knowledge to benefit himself and not to gain personal wealth. It was in an ethos of philosophical thought that the priest looked for another scroll which related the events that took place over a thousand years before his people arrived in Sais in the first place. The original Egyptians who were older than Sais, the "young" cities of Sais was residing in the land and had a conversation with gods. The scroll stated the following: Athena herself had instructed the Egyptians to use the shield and spear and shield, just as they had been taught by the ancient Athenians prior to they arrived. Solon turned to the priest and the priest laughed when he explained to Solon about his own city. "[Athenafounded your state, choosing the location where you were born because she saw there was an environment that was well-mixed and could produce men who were of the highest wisdom."[88

Athena had fought Poseidon to win Athens and it was been a gruelling battle. After the gods won over Titans as well as the Giants and the fierce beast Typhon following the battle, Zeus divided up the earth in lots, and each god were granted lands according to their place within the pantheon. Poseidon Zeus's elder brother, made his way toward Athens and hit the Acropolis using his trident proclaiming it as his as a natural right, and not waiting to see it assigned to the gods. However, Athena was furious. She was aware of the significance of Attica as well as the vast lands Poseidon is likely to be granted at the end of Zeus's judgement This is why she didn't take a smidgen of resentment when they battled.

Poseidon was reckless in defeat and he was not able to comprehend that he was destined to another country, a vast continent that was larger in size than Libya and Asia combined. The it was tucked away behind the majestic Pillars of Hercules. He traveled to it with the speed that a God's voice. He was awed by the beauty and size of the island which extended as far as the naked can see. The priest took the scroll and read the sole description of the continent that been able to survive the 9,000 years of the land of abundance.

"Bordering from the sea and stretching across the island, there was a plain that is believed to have been the most beautiful plain and very fertile in addition, close to the plain, right in its center, in approximately 50 stades, was an edifice that was low from every side. On it lived one of the natives who came out of the ground, Evenor by name, together with his wife Leucippe and as offspring an unborn child, Cleito.

"And the damsel who was at a point of marriageable age her mother died, as did her father; and Poseidon in love with the desire to marry her, tied her. To make the hill on which she resided impervious to attack, he broke the hill all around and created circular zones of land and sea with each one enclosing the other and some were larger, while others were smaller, two from land and three from sea, which he created like a ring from the middle of the island. And the belts were of equal distances from every side, in order to be inaccessible for men as at the time, sailing ships and ships were yet in existence."[99

A godof the sea, Poseidon could visit Cleito at her remote hill at any time he wanted and also devoted much of his energy to this conclusion. The broken-off hill rose out of the huge plane like an enormous pedestal. Poseidon struck the highest edge of the mound two times using his trident. The first strike triggered the gushing stream of ice-cold water that was sweet and nourishing for the mouth. From the second came warm, rich water kind that gods bathed. The two springs dripped through the hills into gullies. They gave a richness to the fertile land which would make the Nile cry out in sorrow and despair.

In the course of Cleito and Poseidon's union Cleito was the father of Poseidon 10 sons and and five sets of twin brothers as well as Poseidon had five sets of twin brothers. Storm God decreed that the continent was to be divided into ten just as he had taken over the island and each one would get their own piece of area where they could settle down and start family members that were theirs. The oldest son was given the center of Atlantis, which was the steep slopes of the huge hill, where Poseidon was to Cleito which was later made the capital of the kingdom. Also, the oldest one, Atlas, gave his name to it as well as the ocean that was surrounding it. "Now on this Atlantis island Atlantis there was an alliance of kings with great and amazing power that ruled over the entire island and also over many other islands as well as parts of the continent. And furthermore, of the land here in the Straits they had a sway over Libya up to Egypt as well as over Europe to Tuscany."[10[10

Thus the ruler of the land was never in need of anything. His family members provided plenty from their allotted areas in the plains. However, everything else he wanted was provided by imports from his expanding empire overseas. The land was a source of olives and wine as well as huge amounts of crops, so much that the Atlantians could have elephants within their territory because this ferocious animal is not able to survive without food.

The priest explained how the area was also abundant in the most precious metals of the time and included the rare "Mountain copper" (Orichalcum) that was as second-highest to gold and not found in the world , except for the stories they were told. The wealth of the land provided the high king and the other tribes all they needed to create an empire which had never existed before and has not been seen for a long time. They began this huge task with a sense of camaraderie, cohesion, the priest told them Solon's Athens could only be an aspirational place.

"First first, they built bridges across the sea's ring which were a part of the old metropolis and created a route to and from the palace of the royal family. They had also built the palace right from the beginning of the city, where it was initially conceived by God as well as their forefathers and as every monarch received it from his predecessor, he enhanced the splendor of the palace and did everything possible to outdo the king who preceded him before finally creating of it a magnificent abode to look at for the size and splendor of the work. Since, starting at ocean, they drilled an entire channel to the circle's outermost part, which was three plethra width, 100 feet deep, and fifty stades long; and they created the entry point to the ocean like an open harbour, by opening the mouth wide enough for the largest ships to sail through.

"Moreover by the land's circles that separated the sea, and atop bridges, they created an opening that ran from circle to circular, sufficient to allow the passage of the trireme in one; and the roofs were erected above to make the sea-side subterranean, as the lip that formed the circles of land were elevated to a enough height over the surface of the sea. The largest circle into the which a drilling was made to the sea was three stades wide and the one of land that was next to it was equally size; while the two circles comprised water, it was two stades wide and the one of dry land was equal in breadth to the previous one of water. Lastly, the circle running around the central island had a stade's width. This island, on which was the royal palace was made up of five stades in the diameter. In addition to the island, the circle and bridge and the plethrum, which was in width, were surrounded around in this direction and the other, by walls of stone and on the bridges that ran along the opposite sides, which were over the sea's passageways they built gates and towers. The stone quarried beneath the central island , all around, as well as from under the inner and outer circles, with some being white, others black and some red. And when they quarried it, they built two docks in the inner area which were hollowed and then roofed with the native stone. Of the structures, some were constructed of a simple color, while in other they woven a pattern of different colours by mixing stones to create a sense of decoration to give the structures an unnatural beauty. They also wrapped with copper, like with plaster, the entire walls' circumference, that was around the outermost circle. And the inner circle they covered with tin and the one that surrounded the acropolis was covered with orichalcum that shimmered like fire."[11[11, 12]

The center of the island on the huge continent that dominated the vast ocean there was a temple dedicated to Cleito and Poseidon the gods of the sea, to whom each of the royal lines paid an annual tribute, and where they honored in memory of their ancestor's Mother and Patron Father. The priest unfolded the scroll once more and described the main shrine that was the temple of the Atlantians as having a touch of a barbaric appearance and the walls were adorned with silver, and the high pinnacles covered in gold. inside the temple, it was filled with gold and ivory, and had plenty of orichalcum. The most sacred sanctuary was a statue of the Sea God driving a chariot that was pulled by six powerful horses and each one with a large wingspan waiting to fly to the skies. Apart from the most revered idol of god and the rest part of the temple lined with statues of heroes, ancestors, and gods and daemons, including those of living princes, surrounded by the sacrifices of people all over the world.

Through the years the twin springs that were located at the acropolis were put for even more purposes, creating bathrooms for the King as well as his princes, and for women and tribesmen and also transformed into lush greenery full of trees, and eventually to the temples of gods as well. In the lush greenery were the exercise areas as well as a fantastic racecourse for the games of the festival in which the people could test their skills against one another and gain fame for their clan before their gods of their ancestors.

Within the vicinity of the garden stood barracks for soldiers. There were strict rules regarding the integration of soldiers and civilians however the most trustworthy officers were granted the privilege of being Royal Guards and then relocated to barracks that were closer to the royal family. Some were even given residences in the Acropolis.

Atlantis The shipyards of Atlantis were loaded with triremes that were fully equipped and the rest of the equipment which made them masters over the oceans. The ocean lapped on the massive exterior wall that rose like it was made by giants. Behind it, homes were constructed right against the battlements since they were confident that the Atlantians had become of their safety. As time passed the main sea-way as well as the biggest harbor swelled with the noise of traders and mariners throughout the day and night. "The entire region sprang out of the ocean to a high point however, the area around the city was just an open plain, wrapping it around and surrounded by mountains that extended all the way to the sea. the plain was level in surface, and was in general rectangular in form, measuring three thousand stades long on each side, and 2000 stades in width in the middle, extending upwards towards sea. The entire region, around the island, looked toward southwards towards the South and was shielded against the Northern blasts."[13[13]

These mountains were unlike anything we see today in their beauty and grandeur and were filled with thriving villages rich thanks to the earth as well as the trees that supplied ample sources for all arts and crafts. There was a massive trench that was constructed in into the center of the plain in which were all the rivers of the island, and also the water they created into a complicated system which they could transport lumber as well as the seasonal crop from the fertile earth of the plains. The produce could feed elephants and armies.

"As regards the manpower of their men it was decided that each allotment be furnished with one person to be the leader of all men within the plain, who were fit to be armed; and the total size of each allotment was around 10 times the number of stades in total, and the number of all allotments was about 60,000; the number of soldiers who lived in the mountains and all the other areas of the land was numerous as per the report. In addition, according to their villages and districts they were given these allotments by their respective leaders.

"So it was decreed that each of the leaders prepare for war with the sixth component of war-chariots's equipment, so as to provide 10,000 chariots, along with two horses and mounted men, as well as two horses that do not have cars, and attached to each one a man equipped with a small shield, and for the charioteer, a rider who jumps between horses as well as two hoplites. archers and slingers; two of each and light-armed slingers as well as javelin-men of three each and four sailors for the manning of 12 hundred ships. This was the military arrangements of the city's royal court; and the rest of the nine were varied in different ways, and it will take quite a while to describe.

"Of the posts and the magistracies of honor, the policy from the beginning of time, was this. The 10 kings was in charge of the men and the majority of the laws were in their specific area and across the city of his home, reprimanding and executing whomever they chose to do so. However, their authority over each other and their relations with each other were guided by the rules of Poseidon which were passed down to them by law and the documents which were engraved by the first princes on an orichalcum pillar and was built in the shrine of Poseidon at the center on the island ... and inscribed on the pillar, in addition to the law as well as an oath, was a vow that brought mighty curses on those who did not abide by ...And there were many more specific laws pertaining to the unique rights of the princes. The most important ones were that they must not fight one another and thatshould someone attempt to take over any city that was their royal residence the princes should be all willing to lend assistance, and consult together, just like their predecessors regarding their strategy in war or other issues, and entrusting the reigns in the royal branch to Atlas and that the king did not have the authority to kill any of his brothers-princes, unless with the agreement by more than half the ten."[14[14]

The king's family, the high king's brothers, as well as the population followed the laws to the letter and despite the riches of their homeland they weren't influenced by it. The inhabitants of the area resisted all activities that didn't aid their progress towards the path of virtue. Contrary to other nations where wealth is amassed by a few to the detriment of all The people of this country broke away from this degrading custom, and by doing this the wealth of the population grew exponentially.

Many people consider the Atlantians as having a moral code to be a result of the divine blood flowing freely and abundantly in their veins. As time passed however, the population became more disengaged from God, both in their blood and in their devotion. The divine light within them waned and became apparent in the gradual decline in their virtues. The population was a massive horde of wretched and ugly in every aspect however the emperors of their empire were impressed by the wealth of their land and believed they were excellent however, the Atlantians suffered from their own degradation.

The first time in a long time since Poseidon gave them wealth The Atlantians were envious and shrewd. They began to look beyond the borders of their empire, and even their allies. They were jealous not of the wealth they could offer however, but for the power that comes with being their own masters. "So this host, all in one place and gathered together, attempted once to subjugate with just one attack our country and yours as well as the entire territory within the Straits."[15The troops were formed battalions. The whole plane was filled in the illumination of the bronze and shouts of incensed soldiers. From the highest point of that continent known as Atlantis, Zeus watched the first battles below. Zeus was witness to the rise and fall of civilizations as the tide of the vast ocean, and he believed that it was the right time to allow Atlantis to begin its descent.

"Wherefore He gathered all gods in the dwelling place that they revere most and sat in the middle of the Universe and observing all the things that are part of generation . After they were all assembled in this manner, he spoke as follows: ..."[16[16.

"And the result was Solon the manhood of your state displayed its strength and courage in the eyes of all of the world. Because it was supreme above the rest in gallantry and martial arts. While acting in part as the leader of the Greeks as well as being on its own, left out by the rest of the people After enduring the most deadly dangers, it defeated the invaders, and raised the trophy, which it rescued from slavery those who were not still enslaved, and those who live within the boundaries of Heracles it was grudgingly released.

"But later on, there came about portentous earthquakes as well as flooding, and a tragic night and day swept their entire human body was washed in the earth and the entire island of Atlantis similarly was submerged by the sea, and then vanished as well. The ocean in that area has become inaccessible and inaccessible due to being clogged by the shoal of that the island produced after it was settling down."[17[17

Plato

Chapter 2: The Antiquated Bust Of Plato

In the narration of the Atlantis story the words "he spoke this way ..." was actually one of the last lines of Plato's Critias which is the "definitive" source for Atlantis. In the Critias that the bulk of the quotations above are found, but as those who have read of the dialogues will know the story ends abruptly. It appears that it was abandoned by Plato one of the first century CE writer Plutarch writing in the Life of Solon, laments the knowledge it could provide. "Plato is a zealous writer who wanted to create and embellish the theme of the lost city of Atlantis as if it were land of an estate, yet aptly his because of a relationship with Solon began his work by laying out magnificent enclosures, porches and courtyards that any story, tale or poem had ever seen before. But he was a bit late in beginning his work, and he died life before completing his work was complete. Thus, the more we take pleasure in what he composed, the more our sadness at the work he did not complete. As we see the Olympieium was located within the city of Athens is the same, so the story about the lost Atlantis with Plato's wisdom Plato is the only of his gorgeous works that remain unfinished."[1818

The bust is of Plutarch

It is essential to situate Critias in a chronology of thought in order to be able to comprehend Plato's motives to mention Atlantis in the first place. To do this, it is essential to revisit Plato's Republic. It was written around. around 380 BCE, Republic is a collection of dialogues written by Socrates and other people concerning their idea of a "perfect social order" in addition to how to define what "justice" can mean. In it, they talk about the various kinds of cities, the ways they're run by the state, and whether they're "good" and "just" and if they are not. They also decided to propose certain possible cities in order to clarify their ideas regarding what the "ideal state" could be.

A fable from the past of Socrates

The "ideal situation" is actually a representation of the ideal state of human consciousness because it was people who realized they could not be self-sufficient that eventually relied on other faculties and eventually the other individuals to build cities-states. The Republic is followed by an argument about the proper way to run the "just" society, and discussing what it means for a society and a person to be just , rather than unfair.

Timaeus recounts the conversation. Socrates and his companions held "day following" the discussion about the ideal state of the Republic It certainly is a continuation of the ideas discussed in the day before. In his ideal state Socrates discusses how citizens should participate in society the manner they feel most comfortable and love the most. He reserves a large portion of society to the "guardians". These guardians are military, and their task is to fight for the city, if needed and, more important, they protect the city from outside enemies. A significant portion of the Republic's work is devoted to the training of guardians, and the way they are governed without law. the city they have too much power at their disposal. Balance is the key to success in promoting morality in the whole population who are encouraged to do the career they want to pursue. Be it priest or guardian or carpenter or philosopher the city-state must be divided into the labor "workforces" that each plays an essential role in society in general.

The main argument in Timaeus is about the nature of all the worlds (both"physical" and "eternal") "physical" as well as"eternal "eternal"), Socrates states that after having spoken about"the "ideal state" He hoped to know what it could be like in an "real-world" setting. "Gladly will I listen to anyone who would describe in words how our State fights against other States in the battles that States fight; in what appropriate a manner it embarks into the battlefield, and how during the midst of war, it displays characteristics like those that are appropriate to its training and education in dealing with state, be it in the form of military action or negotiations with the media. negotiations."[1919

The companions of Socrates wanted the companions of Socrates to "repay" him for his talks earlier in the day by offering some of their own. Hermocrates (one of the companions present) states that Critias spoke of, while they returned home the previous day, a tale "derived from an ancient tradition"[20which could be relevant to the subject of the conversation Socrates would like to listen. "And which was your tale, Critias?" said one of the others. "Its the subject," replied Critias, "was an incredible feat and worthy of being called the most significant of all the exploits that was carried out by the city, Athens, even though the story of it has been lost due to the passage of time and the demise of the people who carried it out." "Tell the world right from to the very beginning,"" she said Amynander, "what Solon related and how did he relate it, as well as those who were the informants who proved the authenticity of the story."

Then, Critias begins to tell the tale of Atlantis in the manner it was revealed by Solon from the priest of wisdom of Sais. The priest extolled the virtues of ancient Athenians, which Solon and other Athenians of the day had lost, and compared their laws to what Solon was able to find in Egypt in the time of his visit. "First is the way it is that the clergy class has been secluded from the other classes and then the craftsmen's class, of which every kind operates on its own, not mixing with other types; and finally the groups of hunters, shepherds and farmers, all distinct and distinct. Additionally the military class here is, as you may have noticed, is held separate from all other classes, and is required by law to devote its entire time to the task of training for battle. A different aspect is the nature of their gear, including spears and shields. For we were among the people of Asia to use these weapons, as it was the goddess who commanded us, just when she instructed you the first of all the inhabitants of the lands of the yonder. In addition, in relation the subject of wisdom, it is easy to can see clearly the law in this case-- how much consideration it has given since the beginning of time in this Cosmic Order, through a thorough understanding of the various effects that divine causes have on the human condition, from divination and the science of medicine, which targets health, and through its mastery of the various other studies. At this time, the Goddess provided you, ahead of everyone else, with the order and routine that she had established, she declared your state, deciding on the place where you were born, as she saw an environment that was well-mixed, and also how it could create men of supreme wisdom."[2121

Egypt was viewed as intelligent and ancient by the ancient Greeks from Solon's time and later, and the parallels between ancient Athenians as well as those who envisioned the "ideal state" described in Republic should not be ignored. The separation of the state and the way in which the military was trained are remarkably identical. Socrates is beginning to learn the idea that "ancient Athens" -- abandoned to the confines erased memory in Greece however, the city is not located in Egypt -was the ideal place they discussed the previous day.

Critias tells the story of Atlantis in the book Timaeus, however, Timaeus is the one who must discuss the origins of the universe first , so that Critias will be able to continue telling the story of "humanity"s actions" following. When Critias starts his recollection of the tale Solon received in the first place, he reminds his listeners that the war among Athens and Atlantis occurred a decade prior to their meeting and they are "kings at Atlantis" are buried under the seas, far over their Pillars of Hercules, "sunk by earthquakes and has formed an impervious mud barrier that prevents people traveling from this point to the oceans beyond from going further."[22When he begins to recount the story, it becomes clear that, similar to the ancient Athenians who were the perfect citizens Socrates would like to meet (and learn about to this day) The later Atlantians who's blood had lost it's "divine spark" through the agesare described as being their exact opposite.

Ancient Interpretations

Chapter 3: A Mid 20th Century Map Showing

Atlantis"Domains

Apart from the statement "derived from ancient traditions," there is little in these texts to suggest Atlantis was anything more than the complete opposite of Socrates's idealistic philosophy. The four words "Atlantis" work difficult, however, in the mindset of a lot of "Atlantists" with whom they have researched and, in some instances have devoted the entirety of their life and wealth to pursuit of a continent that is real. In his book Atlantis at the Sea of Texts, Andrea Albini follows the belief that Atlantis was in fact a creation of Plato's imagination however, he notes that few other authors believe in his. Citing Lyon Sprague de Camp's Lost Continents: The Atlantis Theme in History, Science, and Literature Albini mentions of 216 "Atlantists" who contributed rigorous critical analyses of Plato's writings in where Atlantis appears. But only 37 of them reached the same conclusion like Albini. 23 Albini rejects this information by saying: "The imbalance in favour of those who adhere to the 'geographical theory' is understandable when we consider that those who hold an academic interest in Plato in the field of classical, historical , or philosophical studies aren't likely to take the story of Atlantis seriously enough to dedicate anything more than a solitary reference to it."[2424

The desire to explore Atlantis as a real, historical location it isn't just in the lecture halls of traditional academia This passion isn't a small one. Through the ages There were countless mentions of Atlantis in academic studies, fiction, as well as newspaper articles about treasure hunter real-life characters who put their lives at risk to search for the continent that was never found. As Albini explains, "recurrent themes" in the writings of Atlantis but they at the very minimum reveal some interesting aspects of the authors and their time.

Furthermore, contemporary investigators aren't the first ones to seek out Atlantis. In his book of the same name, The Book of Imaginary Lands, Umberto Eco gives an extremely brief and detailed account on some influential authors about Atlantis. In one section, he points out that for the vast part, the early writers didn't seem to be concerned about the truthfulness of Atlantis the existence of. Aristotle was an alumnus of Plato did not make mention in reference to Atlantis specifically, even though he spoke about the region that was beyond that of the Pillars of Hercules, which he stated that it was just over that India was located. The reason he used to support this claim the possibility that elephants existed on both coasts that is, Africa and India -- and it was evident there was a possibility that "two river systems of the ocean once joined" in some way. Certain scholars consider that this is a vague mention of Plato's Atlantis because Plato was the one to mention that the lost continent as also inhabited by elephants and may serve as a sort of "bridge" that they moved. Aristotle further stated that the regions outside his Pillars of Hercules, or at the very least, parts of that region, was "sheltered from the winds by mud."[26These remarks appear to suggest a presumption about at least a part of the geography taught by his teacher however given that Aristotle doesn't mention Atlantis in any way, there is no reason to believe that he would have taken the tale of war against Athens seriously.

A spry bust from Aristotle

The story and much of the land that was beyond those Pillars of Hercules were questioned in the following centuries however, the idea of a lost "great" world and its people did not completely disappear. The 3rd century CE it was the Roman writer Aelian made fun of Plato's tale by creating one of his islands called Merope that was "beyond that of the Atlantic Ocean" and was packed with huge amounts of wealth and supernatural creatures. [27]

Then came Proclus who was who was a Greek philosopher who wrote during the 5th century of CE. Proclus wrote this of an early fourth century BCE writer Crantor who's writings are only preserved as fragments "With regards to entire narrative about the Atlantics Some say that it's a mere historical record, and that was the view of Crantor who was who was the very first translator of Plato ..."[28[28. Proclus states that Cantor was either in Egypt himself or sent someone else there to conduct a fact-finding expedition and, while there, they were presented with a massive stone on which the account Solon was believed to receive appeared in Hieroglyphs. Proclus offers a different perspective of Cantor with his commentaries, however. "Others also assert that this story is a fable and is a fictional account of events that never had any existence, but that carry to light the natures that are eternal or exist within the universe, not paying attention to Plato who declares "that the story is awe-inspiring in every way, yet is true in every way." Because what is absolutely true does not mean that it is entirely accurate, or even truthful or false in the sense of its apparent meaning truth, but is true according to the meaning that is inwardly derived from it. something of this nature is not completely true."[29[29.

The "inward significance" isn't described in detail and in the passages to follow, Proclus describes how certain observers believed it was an astrological connection to the tale in which the Athenians represent"the "stars" as well as the Atlantians are the "planets" that fight the stars in their circling through the night skies. Overall, Proclus's idea of the reason Plato wanted to include Atlantis wasn't to document the actual events or to elaborate on an underlying philosophical idea and instead, to provide an overall understanding of the universe via the metaphors of the narrative. "[T]he universe is clearly portrayed at the beginning of the dialogue by images. However, in the middle the entire creation of the universe is revealed to us. In the final the partial natures, as well as the extremes of fabrication are interspersed with completes. In the continuation of the discussion regarding a polity, as well as the narrative relating to an Atlantic island, we see by images the theories of the universe. Since if we pay focus to the union and the multitude of everyday things, it is necessary to say that the polity Socrates briefly discusses is a representation of their unity, establishing at its conclusion the unity that pervades everything; however, the war between both the Atlantics against the Athenians as Critias describes in his narrative, is a representation of the division between mundane natures."[3030

He expands upon the symbolic logic by referring to the ancient wisdom and the eminence of Plato and the significance of symbolism in the development and development of soul. "[O]thers think it's presented to us as a representation of the orderly division in the world. Others, as an indicator of the whole of theology. Because it was the norm with the Pythagoreans prior to the advent of scientific thought, to make visible the questions through images and similitudes; and then to introduce them using symbols to give to them with arcane signs. Because, following the stimulation of the intellect of the soul as well as the cleansing of the vision, it's essential to present the entire study of the things that are the subjects of inquiry. This is why the succinct narrative of a polity prior to physiology and physics, place us in the creation of the universe. However, the story of the Atlantics achieves this by symbolism. Because it is typical for stories to communicate a lot of things with symbols. This is why the physiologic aspect is present throughout the dialogue, but in different ways at different locations in accordance with the various ways in which the doctrine is delivered."[31[31

The idea of a symbolism and meaning behind the myth of Atlantis is an idea that would ultimately occupy the minds of many scholars throughout the years to come There were references to this type of thinking in the wake of Proclus. As documented within the written works of 1st century CE geographer Strabo Plato's story was not heavily questioned by the writers of the past. "[T]he legend of that of the Island of Atlantis might be considered to be beyond a simple fiction, since it was told by Solon according to basis of Egyptian priests that this island, which was as big as an entire continent, was once present, even though it was disappeared."[3232

In the majority of cases and definitely for the majority times during the Medieval Period, scholars did not want to read too much into the story of Plato beyond the truthfulness of the continent's past existence. Remarks on Atlantis generally were used to strengthen their own theories about geography or claims to Earth that was flat (as for instance in the story of the 6th century CE Christian writer Cosmas Indicopleustes). The motives of Proclus to discredit Plato's tale as"fable "fable" as well as to praise the fable as a philosophical blessing to mankind will not be seen again for many centuries.

The Renaissance

Of all the significant historical events of the Renaissance There was one that was likely to have a profound impact on an European views more profoundly than the others. It was, of course discovering the New World.

Following Christopher Columbus' discovery of the Americas in 1492, and the subsequent contacts Europeans made with the and culturally (and economically) prosperous Mayan as well as Aztec peoples during the time which followed, there appeared an explosion of interest in new civilizations. Naturally, this resulted in an increase in curiosity about Atlantis and, more specifically an extension of Plato's tale to the Americas.

The reason was a growing interest in "New" in addition to "Old" realms. While the New World promised riches that went beyond the expectations of European rulers, kings and despots however, the Renaissance opened the door to the past too and the past provided the possibility of a different kind of wealth. When Constantinople was taken over by the Ottomans in the middle of the 15th century scholars, translators and academics of all sorts fled to the west with their ideas , and most importantly earlier translations of the philosophers' works have shaped the modern world so profoundly. Because of the generous support by the Medici family in Florence modern translations into Latin -the language of the time and led to revolutionary developments in political and philosophical thinking. Cosimo di'Medici snatched copies of the entire collection of Plato's published works, and immediately set up a translator work in translating the works into Latin.

Cosimo di' Medici

The translator was Marsilio Ficino. Marsilio Ficino was a 15th century scholar who is acknowledged as among the top individuals within the modern "Humanist" movement as well as an emergence of Neoplatonism at the time despite the fact that the man was an ordained Catholic priest. He revived the Plato's "Academy" at Florence using the Medici family's permission and funds and funding, and it was at this point that Ficino began to study Plato's work.

Ficino

In relation to Atlantis, Ficino pointed out an inconsistency between Plato's words: "[W]henever he imagines something it is his custom to label it an fable, However, in this case (in Critias) he does not hesitate to label it history."[33He also made reference to the exact phrase used by Proclus in relation to the story that took place in Atlantis being "surprising to the point of absurdity, but absolutely real." His translation was the principal source of information for scholars from all over Europe fascinated by Plato's works that bolstered the conclusions that Ficino arrived. After a few decades, scholars like Girolamo Fracastoro, Giovanni Battista Ramusio, Pedro Sarmiento de Gamboa as well as Francisco Lopez de Gomara all believed in the Ficino claims that the tale was not just a fairy tale, but was real. Lopez de Gomara, in his History of the Indies, even wrote that the design of the "New Lands" corresponded to Plato's description in boldly asserting that Aztecs were the missing peoples of Atlantis. Over the centuries that followed, the claim that the Aztecs as well as those of the Mayan populations were "lost individuals" of Atlantis was to gain traction.

However some scholars did not lend their full faith in Ficino's assertions of veracity. For instance in her book Ficino in Spain the historian Susan Byrne draws attention to the scholar of the 16th century Francisco Cervantes' doubts. "All writers on Plato affirm that this story is definite and accurate to the point that the majority particularly Marsilio Ficino as well as Platina are unable to acknowledge an interpretation that is not literal, though some affirm this that they do, that is what Marsilio himself writes in his "Annotations on the Timaeus'. Thus, we can conclude that this is the case and that it is true, who can not believe that this island of Atlantis was founded in the Straits of Gibraltar, or just a little after Cadiz began, later extended and continued across this vast gulf from which point it extended it extended to both the south and north as well as to the West and east, did it have the potential to be larger that Asia and Africa?"[3535

Others went further, denying the truthfulness of an "real" Atlantis, such as the French philosopher Michel de Montaigne, who wrote in the 16th century "Plato makes Solon to tell him that he'd learned from the priests from at the Citie in the Says in Aegypt and that, prior to and prior to the general Deluge there was a vast region known as Atlantis located near the mouth of the Strait of Gibraltar and containing more land that was more stable that Affrike as well as Asia combined ... However, there was no striking look to it. of the said Iland could be the modern world we've just found out about; as it was not far from having reached Spaine and had an amazing effect of flooding to be able to take away over twelve hundred leagues in the way we perceive it. In addition the fact that our modern Navigations are now beginning to realize that it's not an Iland it is a more solid land and also a continent."[36[36.]

Michel de Montaigne

The Head Chronicler for the Indies, Antonio de Herrera y Tordesillas who wrote around the same timeframe as de Montaigne rejected the idea that there was a continent lost, when Cervantes de Salazar's writings with the basic words "this is an fable."[3737

But, for the vast majority during the period of 16th-century there were a few who doubted Plato's tale and less that believed it was an analogy similar to the one Plato used when writing. Byrne also brings the reader's focus to the contemporary of Cervantes de Salazar Pedro Sarmiento de Gamboa, an explorer and polymath from Spain who claimed that the tale was given by "the godlike Plato" and claimed that it was an "marvelous story filled with truth."[3838

Ficino's remarks, enhanced by his academic reputation as well as his discovery of The New World, and the endless possibilities for suppositions therein attracted the attention of the best writers of the time and led to an empirical approach to The Lost Continent. Sir Thomas More published one such inspired work in 1516 titled Utopia. The title came of The Greek term "topos" which means "place" also known as "locale" which is followed by an uncertain "u". The confusion of the "u" is within its Greek prefixes "eu" which means "good" as well as "ou" which renders the word negative, which means "non-place" or "nowhere." Within the text, More explores the dialogue of Socrates and his fellow travelers in Republic, Timaeus, and Critias as portrayed in the complete Version of the title, On the Most Perfect kind of Republic and About the New Island of Utopia. In his classic publication, More describes a theoretical island where the ideal social practices, like the military, government and the religion, are implemented in "real-life" situations, exactly as Socrates wanted to hear the conversations of his fellow citizens from Timaeus as well as Critias.

Sir Thomas More

In 1623 Sir Francis Bacon's incomplete book, New Atlantis, was published after his death.

The novel Bacon describes an unnamed island known as Bensalem that is located away from Peru and has some of the traits of the beginning of Plato's Atlantis as well. They are honest and wise regardless of their wealth, but they're also religious as they received an original version of the Bible as well as an inscription to Saint Bartholomew miraculously many years prior to the time the fictitious Europeans arrived on the enigmatic island. The islanders are, as the book states, prefer to be hidden from the all world, and only interact with it through sending scholars out to collect data that they later utilize in their own technologically advanced research. The idea of a perfect society the lost "Eden" is highlighted. A perfect society, governed by a perfect society and culture, whose existence was lost to mystery of time, intrigued writers across Europe It was this obsession about "lost perfectionism" that prompted the next research and writings about Atlantis.

Sir Francis Bacon

From the Renaissance from the Renaissance onwards and onward, the continent of Atlantis began to shine as a source of fascination for those looking to discover and, in some cases to justify the anciently or superiority of a particular current "people". To analyze and explain these claims will require several volumes and, in the end yield little more than the incredibly enjoyable task of following the trail of breadcrumbs they had diligently placed behind them.

The notion to be an "heir" to the Atlantian history, or more commonly, "bloodline", became quite commonplace during the nationalist enthusiasm that swept through the country following the Renaissance. At the end of 17th-century, Swedish scientist Olof Rudbeck wrote a 2,500-page essay about the "true" place of Atlantis in his homeland of Sweden. Rudbeck gave an etymological "proof" for his hypothesis in his Atlantis Man's Home. He claimed that the great-grandson of Noah left towards Sweden in search of a better life. He also claimed that Nordic runes were predated by the Phoenician script, which influenced the Indo-European languages and consequently, Swedish was the original "Language from Eden". [39]

Rudbeck

While these assertions may seem absurd in the present, the demand to have the creation of an Atlantian geography or a genealogy (or both) seems to have resounded in the minds of a lot of serious scholars during both the late 17th and early 18th century, as well. Umberto Eco described how the historian and philosopher Giambattista Vico decried the zeitgeist in his 1744 publication, Principles of the New Science. "Having begun the subject We will give an outline of the views that have been formulated in regards to it , opinions that are so ambiguous or sloppy and smug and so many that we don't need to discuss them. ..."

Vico was then critical of the notions that Goths were the first Atlantians and that they were the preservers of "the letters that were divinely created through Adam," and that Dutch was the "mother of all languages" and was passed down since the beginning of time by Atlantians. He then is at Rudbeck, "who will have it that the Greek letters originated from runes, and they claim that Phoenician lettering ... could be described as reversed runes, And that Greeks then straightened them up here and then rounded them up there with compass and rule. The inventor is referred to as Merkurssman in the Scandinavians and he is a Merkurssman, he will also have it that Mercury who invented the letters specifically for Egyptians was the son of a Goth."

Vico

There was another group of scholars who claimed that the place of Atlantis was not within their own country but was within the territories of other nations. It included Athanasius Kircher, who put the island within the Canary Islands, while Jean-Sylvain Bailly believed Atlantis was situated within Iceland, or Greenland. Voltaire believed that it was the island of Madeira as well as Bartolomeo de Las Casas believed that the Atlantians were the ancient civilization of Israel. F.C. Baer who linked Atlantis destruction with the destruction at Sodom And Gomorra. [40]

A work from 1882 titled Atlantis: The Antediluvian World was written by an American known as Ignatius Donnelly who Eco described in a reasoned manner as "the writer who, more than anyone else, has revived his version of the Atlantis legend." Donnelly was a U.S. Congressman and amateur scientist who was famous for his pseudo-histories about his theories about the "true writership" of Shakespeare's plays, as well as the history and origins of Atlantis. From the line Eco uses from his account of the very beginning of Atlantis it appears that Donnelly did not only adopt the theories that had been previously proposed for Atlantian genealogy, but also committed himself to constructing an all-encompassing theory of an era-old culture that was rooted in that obscure island.

Donnelly

In the absence of pseudo-history, Donnelly's genuine enthusiasm about Atlantis and its impact on modern culture is a bit charming.

"There was once within the Atlantic Ocean in the Atlantic Ocean, just opposite at the entrance of the Mediterranean Sea, a large island that was the remains of the Atlantic continent, is known to the world of ancient times as Atlantis. The description of the island provided to Plato does not represent, like it is widely believed, a fable but a true story. Atlantis was the place that man first rose from the ashes of barbarism and then civilisation. It was, over the course of time massive and populous nation, with overflowing waters that spanned were the shores of Gulf of Mexico, the Mississippi River, the Amazon and The Pacific Coast and the Pacific coast of South America, the Mediterranean and West Coast in Europe and Africa and the Baltic and the Black Sea and the Caspian were populated by civilised peoples. It was the real Antediluvian world, it was the Garden of Eden; the Gardens of the Hesperides; the Elysian Fields; the Gardens of Alcinous The Mesomphalos; Olympus; the Asgard of the ancient cultures of the ancient nations representing the universal memories of a vast place where people of the past lived for centuries with peace and happiness.

"The gods and goddesses from the early Greeks as well as the Phoenicians and the Hindus along with the Scandinavians were just the heros, kings and queens of Atlantis as well as the actions associated with them in mythology are an ambiguous recall of actual historical events. Mythology from Egypt and Peru was the source of the first religion of Atlantis and was sun-worship. The first colony established in the time of the Atlanteans was likely to be located in Egypt which was a copy of that from that of the Atlantic island. The tools of the Bronze Age of Europe originated from Atlantis. Atlantis was the place where iron was first discovered. Atlanteans weren't the only producers of iron. It is believed that the Phoenician Alphabet, parent of all European alphabets, came of an Atlantean alphabet, and was also transferred by Atlantis towards people of the Mayas from Central America. Atlantis was the first home for Atlantis was the seat of Aryan or Indo-European family of nations and also of peoples of the Semitic populations, as well as perhaps as well from those of the Turanian races. Atlantis lost its inhabitants in a tense natural quake, where the entire island was submerged into the ocean and nearly all of its inhabitants. Some people escaped aboard rafts and ships and took across the world in the west and east of the horrific catastrophe which is still remembered to this day current time as part of stories of the Flood and Deluge myths of the various countries of The Old as well as the New Worlds."[4141

According to Donnelly that is, there were a few civilizations that weren't influenced by the Atlantian beauty, but Eco dispels the mystery declaring "All the myths and legends are built on the assumption that ziggurats and pyramids can be located in Egypt as well as the Middle East as well as in different Asiatic or Amerindian civilisations. This isn't a lot since structures built on mounds may be developed independently by different cultures since they reflect the way that sand accumulates due to wind motion and stepped structures are usually the result of erosion, and the design of trees may be a clue to the shape of the column wherever."

Despite Donnelly's idea that of an Atlantis that influenced a variety of world civilizations certain thinkers of the 20th century reduced his vision to a narrower scope. People such as Alfred Rosenberg would see in Atlantis the pureness that of the "unblemished" race that he always dreamed of. In his dreamy mind, Rosenberg "found" Atlantis under the huge Atlantic icebergs. There, an old "master race" was dormant, waiting for the right moment to reveal its shining glory as heroes that resembled Nietzsche's "ubermensch" to the world. It was true that Rosenberg identified this group as "a ancient Nordic culture" who's physical power and mental agility above other "mixed" races that he encountered everywhere he went during the 20th century.

Rosenberg continued to be influential with the Nazi party during the years that followed as a theorist as well as an influential party member.

Rosenberg

Chapter 4: Research Interest

The 19th and 18th centuries witnessed some of the most significant advances in the field of science and technology. Like Charles Darwin and Alexander von Humboldt were pioneers of rationalism as well as discovery and it was through their research that Atlantis came back into mind of elite. The earth's age and the position and forms of the continents led scientists to look at their ideas about the "lost" continents in the record of history with a very thoughtful and thoughtful way.

The Atlantic Ocean captured the attention of a lot among these researchers, among them one of them, the French naturalist Georges-Louis Leclerc, Comte de Buffon who saw in that vast expanse among continents the distinctive shadows of the forgotten continent that once connected the two. Buffon claimed that the areas that surround the ocean -- specifically Ireland, America, and the Azores -were the last traces of the continent, with its outer edges left following the time the smaller rings on the island been submerged by the waves. [42 The Renaissance theories on Aztecs and Mayans

Mayans along with the Aztecs were eventually taken up by Buffon as well as one of the Prussian researcher Alexander von Humboldt, whose explorations of the Amazon resulted in his thoughts on these topics. But, the brilliant scientists were hesitant to come up with concrete theories regarding Atlantis beyond the mere mentions of conversation in their correspondence. [43]

The concept of cataclysmic catastrophes became popular in a few scientific circles in between the 19th and 18th century. Many scientists turned to books written by Athanasius Kircher, and in his writings they discovered the scientific basis for. "A Land," Kircher wrote, "call'd Atlantis, seems to have been swallowed due to no other cause However, the repercussions from these earthquakes and fires then arising. Even to this day there are tracts that are filled with fires and flames that are bursting out of their underground storehouses. The violent and fury that as well Columbus and Vespuccius and Vespuccius, in their greatest danger, experienced." In the time of his, Ignatius Donnelly had spread theories about the catastrophic events of history, notably those of the telluric "impacts" from extraterrestrials as well as it was the French naturalist Georges Cuvier developed a theory in the same vein at the start of the 19th century. Cuvier reported a massive cataclysmic incident in the Pacific Ocean off the coast of Siberia and Siberia, where a huge number of trees that were not native to the region were found to have been removed out of the ground by an flood of some sort and then kept 200 feet below to the level of earth. Geology was able to revive Plato's tale once more.

In fact, Charles Darwin became embroiled in the haze of a new period in Atlantian interest. There were some theories that the similarities between Miocene plants from Europe and modern plants from easterly states within the U.S. was due to these plants moving thousands of years earlier across a continent that was lost located in the Atlantic. Darwin thought about these claims and went so to conduct tests on seeds to find out whether they had sprouted after being exposed to the ocean. After he realized this was the case but he then spent less time discussing the topic of a rumored missing Atlantian continental "bridge."[45The bridge was a rumor that he had come across.

Scientists and treasure hunters have read the works of Plato in the same way as they have searched across the globe, but no one has been successful yet. Theories that claim to locate Atlantis within The U.S., Peru, the Caribbean as well as West Africa, among others have their fans However, the one place that has been causing controversy isn't located "beyond beyond Pillars of Hercules" that the majority of people are familiar with. Many have instead focused on the Island that is Santorini (ancient term "Thera") located in the Aegean Sea. is located on the Aegean Sea, about 130 miles away from the Greek mainland.

In the second millennium BCE during the second millennium BCE Minoan Empire was massive naval power that controlled a large portion of the inhabitants on the island of Crete which was its base. In the second millennium BCE, Greek cities, which included Athens and Athens, had been "Cretanized," as historian Robert Graves refers to it at some point in around the end of the 1800s BCE. [46 The Cretan empire was able to incorporate cities with incredible speed during this period however, it was not a "velvet revolution." Cities were able to resist and resisted throughout the Greek mainland and islands of the Mediterranean and evidence of this can be found in the legend of Atlantis.

It is believed that the Minoan Empire eventually came to its end, as many researchers believe, because of an immense volcanic eruption located on the Island of Thera about 1500 BCE. The eruption was more than 10 times stronger than the one in Krakatoa in 1883. It could result in a huge tsunami that could have reached as far as 40 miles to the north of Crete. An archaeologist Sandy MacGillivray, who worked on the excavations that took place on this island in Santorini described "The Minoans were so confident of the navy they had that they wereliving in unprotected towns across the entire coastline. Then, you travel to Bande Aceh [in Indonesia, where the tsunami ravaged] of the 2004 tsunami and find that the rate of mortality is around 80 percent. If we're looking at the same mortality rate, then that's the ending of the minoans."

With the strength of the navy of this advanced civilization, in addition to its massive dimension and shape Minoans are being painted using their Atlantian brush over the last few times. There are, naturally many unanswered questions or not addressed to the delight of the majority of historians. One of them is what was the date Atlantis was believed to have existed at around. 9600 BCE and has since been contested with the assertion that it was a mistake of the interpretation Plato received, which mistook the number 900 years for 9,000 years. The place "beyond that of the Pillars of Hercules" has been challenged with the notion that this name is assigned to various sites in the ancient world typically straits or islands like that in the region between Sicily as well as mainland Italian mainland. But, this idea has been a hotly debated topic for centuries, and geographer Strabo wrote about his Pillars as being in an island in the Strait of Gibraltar. However there are many who consider the mythical civilization to be part of the art, history and minoan culture.

Chapter 5: Plato's Atlantis

> Origins

Ade popularized by Plato The verifiable account of Atlantis actually comes from Solon the fourth Plato's incredible granduncle who was an Athenian politician who lived between 664 to 560 BC. Solon himself did not ever deliver any publicity and was believed by many to be gay. However, his younger brother Dropides became Plato's fourth great granddad, who was the one to which Plato was able to acquire Solon's original manuscripts. Solon engaged in the tale of Atlantis while visiting the revered minister of Sais which was a major city located in northern Egypt. The revered minister who Solon received the authentic information about Atlantis was known as Sonchis the person accountable for the direction of Sais's Temple of Athena at Sais and also arranging the chronicled documents that were found in the archives of the sanctuary.

Table 1. Genealogy from Plato to Solon

Dropides

(Brother to Solon). Solon)

I

The Elder I, ritias

Leaides I

ritias the younger I

Glaucon I

erictione I

lato

Illustration 2 Illustration 2: Illustration 2: School of Athens, showing the principal scholars of the ancient style Greek artifacts, among whom are Plato as well as Solon.

Solon

A concise sketch of Solon can be useful in understanding the origins of Plato's knowledge about Atlantis. Solon was introduced to the world in the year 640 BC in Salamis the scion of the distinct Eupatrid group who enjoyed Attican respectability. According to historical family documents that the Eupatrids were patrilinealy evicted from King Codrus who was the ruler between 1089 and 1068 BC as the final lord of Athens before a more conservative form of government was established within the city-state.

Solon's early life was marked by his unwavering devotion to God and a strong dedication to his affluent mother. The family was shocked by the fact that Solon was able to choose an occupation in opposition to the family's wishes. Undoubtedly, he caused some anger for his shrewdly conceived mother, Solon was able to choose the wrong career path in the field of business. It was a long time later however, in aftermath of amassing an impressive fortune, the mother's concerns were not entirely satisfied.

alleviated.

having made his fortune in the business world, Solon was chosen boss justice of Athens

In 594 BC. The following year Solon was able to defeat an attack in 594 BC on his Athenian island Salamis and earned him more praise from the masses. Following the military's successful encounter in Salamis, Solon arranged an obligation-related celebration in Athens in which all resident's obligations waived. Afraid of retribution of the town's fiscal at the top, and nearing the end of his tenure as the city's chief official, Solon chose to leave Athens and go into self-imposed exile. He sailed for Egypt first, before arriving in Sais and stayed there through a long time. It was during this time within Sais that Solon began to meet Sonchis and by her was granted access to the sanctuary libraries, where the written records of Atlantis were stored.

Illustration 3 Illustration 3: the Battle of Salamis, where Solon led the Athenians to victory.

The gyptian advancement of humankind protected the Atlantean records for a long time following Atlantis was destroyed. It appears that Solon was not able to find the Atlantean documents in the massive sanctuary library accidentally. Instead, the Atlantis account was brought out to the public by Sonchis in a deliberate manner. Sonchis asserted the idea that Atlantis was the first and oldest link in the history of Greek development, discovered it

It was a surprise that Egyptians have more information on the early stage of the time of

Greece than those who were actually Greeks. Similar to how Muslim researchers contributed to protecting Europe's experiences through The Dark Ages for resulting renewed introduction to Europe in the Renaissance as well, Egyptian advancements help preserve Greek culture after the demise of Atlantis.

Following his stay after his time in Egypt, Solon set out to Cyprus and was able to gain the service of the head of Cyprus as an overseer of the development projects for the newly-established Cypriot capital. Solon took a short trip back to Athens and, once more, was involved in political conflict that forced him to retreat to Cyprus to protect himself. Perhaps it was in this brief trip back to Athens the time that Solon abandoned his Atlantis compositions in the home of his parents. The original copy of the manuscript could be later purchased by Plato and would become the basis of the creation of his Atlantis chronicle.

Solon was in Cyprus throughout the remainder of his life and never returning to Athens. The latter years of his life were spent writing poetry and giving philosophical advice. For example, Solon was tasked with providing direction on behalf of the king Croesus of Lydia, a kingdom situated in Asia Minor, on philosophical matters. Solon was disappointed to learn that the lord who was famous for being the most lavish man on earth at the time, also believed that he was the most cheerful person on earth. Bestricken by his arrogance to the max, Solon forewarned the ruler with the wise words "count no man satisfied until his death in the event that luck would could betray his sudden. It was a while after the kingdom was attacked by Persians and awaiting execution at the tree of the hangman in Persepolis and King Croesus was reported to have said "I should have been paying close attention Solon."

Olon was a well-known scholar during his final years in Cyprus. His apothegms and works were are widely known throughout the Hellenic world and he was regarded as part of the Seven Sages of Greece whose compositions were highlighted on pages from the Oracle of Delphi. Solon died in a state of utter poverty, unmarried and without children, in the Greek island in Cyprus around 560 BC aged 80 years. Solon was burned to death and his remains scattered across Salamis the island where his birth.

>> Sonchis of Sais

The story from Sonchis from Sais is essential to the story of Atlantis because the office he worked for is believed to be responsible for protecting the narrative evidence of Atlantean development for those who will be living in the future. Sonchis came into this world at Sais, Lower Egypt along the Canopian banks of the Nile River. While the precise date of his entry into the world is not known He was believed to be in his 80s when Sonchis was born.

met Solon in 590 BC. His date of birth in the 670s BC. Sonchis was part of a family of anglers. As a youngster was a child, he played in water from the Nile with a kayak cut by his father, launching nets in the water's depths. As the child grew into a young man it was evident that he was bound to something more significant than being an angler. A well-educated and competent man Sonchis was taken to close Egyptian Theological and cloister school in order to be trained to join the group. Sonchis got a job in the Egyptian ministry in 700 BC at the age of 20. His appointment was the beginning of a highly productive and well-educated sixty-year-old vocation to the Egyptian priesthood.

In the early days of his service, Sonchis was shipped off Heliopolis to Heliopolis, where he studied under the guidance of Psenophis the revered minister renowned for his academic dedication and discipline. At Heliopolis, Sonchis concentrated on the historical background of Egyptian human progress as well as his study of the Atlantean realm. Sonchis was extremely knowledgeable about this series of events that he was allowed through the consecrated priest of Heliopolis to remove his Atlantis Codex from the Temple of Heliopolis and take this to the Temple of Athena at Sais to take care. Sonchis successfully argued that a diary that is so crucial to the start of Greek human development should be preserved in a sanctuary dedicated to an Greek goddess, not in the temple of Heliopolis that was dedicated to the worship of an Egyptian god. The fact that Psenophis accepted Sonchis' plea to bring at least the Atlantis Codex to the Temple of Athena is a clear proof for its protection of those who would be the next generation of Greeks.

Illustration 4 Illustration 4: Temple of Athena at Sais in the Sais area, in which Sonchi's Atlantis Codex was kept.

Hesiod is the First Greek writer to address Atlantis?

Hesiod The father of Greek poetry, was born to the world in Boetia, Greece around 740 BC He was the eldest child of a wealthy migrant who came from Asia Minor. In a bizarre way, Hesiod's father chose to pay the family's massive fortune through his

younger young child Perses more youthful child, Perses Hesiod in regard to his Will. With no attractive legacy upon which to rely, Hesiod had to make his living as the ancients did through the sweat of his temple. Being an educated Greek the aristocrat was common for Hesiod to become an essayist. From the beginning, Hesiod had partaken in poetry competitions across Greece including the most well-known contest that was held in Euboea every year, and where He won ahead of all the others in the contestants. Although many significant works can be attributable to

Hesiod but the most significant of them can be found in the Theogony. The Theogony is a epic sonnet, which depicts the events and parentage of the Greek divinities. In general, Hesiod is believed to have invented what the name of fifty ocean sprites that were clearly created by the ocean god Nereus.

The Theogony, Hesiod depicts the brutal destruction of a major city due to an internal conflict between Greek gods. Although it is not clear if the previous work by Hesiod really refers to Plato's Atlantis There are a lot of similarities. Prior to Solon's work, Hesiod depicts an old city that was shaken by violent disruption. The image sounds like volcanic, and it echoes from the Thera eruption of 1600 BC. As stated by Hesiod who was the one to tell the date Thera was destroyed

"The vast expanse of the ocean was reverberating violently and the Earth was roaring with fury, the vastness of the sky shaken and groaned. A massive trembling sank into the dark depths of Tartarus with a sharp, piercing rumble creating a massive roll of hallowed flame. Lands that were ripe throughout the area fell apart as they burned, and massive backwoods roared in the flame.

The entire Earth as well as the sea and the deserted ocean began to rise. A massive fire was sparked into the air, so the hot air enveloped the Titans. The view there was to be seen and the roar to hear made it appear as if Earth and the vast sky above were colliding. It was as if Earth was being crushed, and like the sky was crashing downwards upon her. The wind added to the chaos, whirling dust about, accompanied by incredible Zeus thunderous volleys and slowing down. The gods fought with determination throwing the stones at 300 in a steady stream with the force of their enormous hands until they obscured Titans with a cloud of rockets. The incredible Earth created 100 snake heads that had glowing dark tongues and ablaze of fire. The earth was ablaze with huge amounts of it. were smoldering under the heat of the immense heat and dissolving the tin that was heated up in cauldrons in shapes by skilled workers and, like iron, the most grounded metal and melted by the heat of the flames in a cut in the mountain." Does this image of the Theogony depict the destruction of Atlantis or is it merely unsubstantiated? The author is of the opinion that the depiction is not credible enough to make any definitive conclusions about it, and most likely doesn't refer towards Plato's Atlantis. The word Atlantis is not mentioned anywhere in the Theogony so it might be reasonable to consider the erroneous notion that the Theogony is not in any way connected with Atlantis aside from addressing an old tale of a dreadful meteorological anomaly. The credit for preserving memories of Atlantis for those who will come in the future who follow this path does not lie with Hesiod but it is with Solon or Sonchis.

Illustration 5. The demise of Atlantis.

Chapter 6: Alternative Hypotheses

The main reason behind this publication lies in the need to prove that Plato's Atlantis is a reference to the Minoan Atlantean kingdom with its capital in Santorini which existed in the original records of approximately 3000 BC up to about 1600 BC. However, in the event that this translation is correct is not the only one, and the book will also look at different views. Some historians have, for instance, believed the possibility that Plato's Atlantis refers to a lost world-wide phenomenon that existed between 10,000 BC and was also destroyed by a global catastrophe. This theory is based on the belief that the ocean's levels from nowhere grew, causing massive flooding of areas of beaches around the globe exactly 12,000 years earlier than at the end period of Younger Dryas, a period that is among the series of historical events that are notable for the massive glaciation that occurred in the northern part of the world. The rise in ocean levels is believed to be due to a massive bolide that caused the ice sheets to melt on the northern hemisphere of the equator, generating massive amounts of heat and energy. The ice sheets were able to disintegrate and levels in the ocean to rise within the land squint of the eye. The meltwater, as it was said, caused floods of a large and a beach front development that was globally in its reach. It was suggested by the well-known author Graham Hancock and others that this advancement of mankind could be Plato's Atlantis.

The existence of an older all-world civilization is confirmed to a certain degree by archeological evidence. In this case, for instance the recent discovery from Gobleke Teppe in Turkey, an enormous complex that encompasses exactly 200 huge T-shaped designs indicates that the remains of human development began to surface as at the time of the year 10,000 BC within the Near East. It's therefore not unreasonable to think to believe that the impact of bolide that occurred around 12,000 years BP that melted and melted the Eurasian as well as North American ice covers may certainly have caused flooding in a seaside speculative human progress that was in place in the present.

The possibility that the flood of an unknown early stage advancement may have occurred in the year 10,000 BC caused through frosty meltwater accompanied by a bolide sway isn't in doubt. The issue however the fact that this advancement of humans was like Plato's Atlantis. The theory could be confined for a long period of time. For starters according to Sonchis of Sais who is the person who kept the Atlantis Codex, the lost development to Atlantis could be described as Greek in

character. There is no evidence to suggest it that Greek development was in existence prior to 10,000 BC. It is also impossible to believe that Stone Age records tracing all up to 10,000 BC could have been found in the past Egypt at the time of the appearance of Solon in the year 600 BC. Take a look at how little we know of the existence of the planet just 3000 years ago. For instance, scientists for a long period of time have had a hard time finding dates that are reliable to Abraham and Moses who are two of the most important patriarchs in the biblical story. Also, think about how dependent science today is on archeological discoveries that were embraced in the twentieth century to form the vast majority of information discovered on the past civilizations. Before the twentieth century for instance, King Tutankhamen as well as Minoan Greece were completely unknown to scientists. Are there any chances that the real facts regarding the Stone Age development from 10,000 BC could have been discovered in ancient Egypt during the period of about 600 BC at the time Solon was still there? It seems to be all except for the incomprehensible. Thirdly, there are a myriad of plausible explanations as to the reason that Plato's Atlantis refers to the Mediterranean domain , with its capital located on Santorini, the Greek island Santorini which was flourishing during the second millennium BC which was just a couple of hundred years prior to the time of Solon. The antiquated realm has left many permanent trails throughout the Mediterranean district that can be observed to the present day.

> An Atlantis located in southern Spain

The possibility of the possibility that Atlantis is a city that was located in southern Spain was suggested by Dr. Richard Freund, an educator in Judaic Studies in the University of Hartford. The educator Freund states that the principalstays of Hercules depicted in the works of Plato throughout his Dialogs refer towards that of the Straits of Gibraltar, not the Pillars of Hercules which outline the Laconian inlet. Freund's knowledge of the region and Hercules' Pillars of Hercules has driven him to search for antiquated Atlantis in the southern part of Spain.

According to the work of Freund, the location of Plato's Atlantis is located in the southern part of Spain in the Donana National Park close to Seville. The park's public nature is known due to its wild ponies as well as the an immense riparian ecosystem that extends across many miles. In the last quarter of 2003, archeologists noticed the deserted seaside areas close to Seville had striations of roundabouts in the form of a scene that resembled Plato's representation of Atlantis. Freund immediately seized upon this idea and organized an archeological mission at the public park to find the remains of the city that was lost.

Freund developed a smart method of examining the subsurface of the earth using electromagnetic waves to determine if any of the covered designs existed deep beneath. The multidisciplinary team of researchers who examined the region found several massive agglomerations stone, which could be evidence of the emergence of structures, which are located beneath the outer layer of Donana estuary. Freund believed that these stone patterns could be remains that were left behind from Atlantean temples.

His trip to explore southern Spain came up with a couple of delightful findings. In one instance, his team discovered a puppet dating back to 4400 years from The Phoenician goddess Aphrates showing the evidence of a Phoenician presence in the area from between 2400 and 2400 BC. Despite the discovery of the teacher, there were no rare finds of ancient origin that have a Minoan-Atlantean origin were discovered. The teacher suggested that the presence of humans in southern Spain that he discovered could be the final remnants of the city mentioned in the scriptural book of Tarshish that is depicted within The Old Testament Book of Chronicles and the Book of Kings. The theory was to be the case that Tarshish and Atlantis could be one in the identical.

In spite of Professor Freund's translation in all likelihood the old city he discovered within southern Spain was actually a western station within the MinoanAtlantean kingdom in the opposite case, it was a Phoenician province. There isn't any evidence to suggest the possibility that Plato's Atlantis was located in Spain. Additionally, despite extensive electromagnetic underground plans and underground structures, none with Minoan-Atlantean designs were discovered. Spain isn't the most likely site to find Plato's Atlantis.

Atlantis of Mauritania Atlantis of Mauritania

The Richat Structure located in Northern Mauritania is without doubt the most plausible explanation for the existence of Atlantis in North Africa. The Richat Structure is a 23-mile wide area of land that is arranged in concentric circles on the farthest portion in the Mauritanian desert. The structure is located just 400 miles away far from Atlantic Ocean, but straight patterns in the sand surrounding the structure show that torrential movements impacted the area around 12,000 years ago.

Richat Structure Richat Structure is steady with Plato's Atlantis in a variety of ways. For starters it is precisely aligned with the elements of Plato's Atlantis and is the result of a record of errors in the text. The geophysical form of the structure is made up of raised ground separated by lower despondencies, giving the appearance of canals with water.

creating circular circles on land. According to certain researchers in the past, the main island within the Richat Structure would have housed the Atlantean Temple of Poseidon and the largest circle surrounding the island was home to an Atlantean sleeper enclosure for the military as well as drydocks that were used by warships. The largest channel within the Richat Structure was said to be the site of the Atlantean maritime armada , which consisted of more than 1000 warships. The armada would travel through the region of the inward channel and was protected by the strategic island for repairs and maintenance.

The underground water table that surrounds The Richat Structure is likewise fascinating. Up to a depth that is 600 feet deep, the entire region's water table is essentially salt water. The island in the inward part within the Richat Structure is the main region of a freshwater spring throughout the entire district. It is estimated that the sanctuary of Poseidon was built over this freshwater source on the island in the back due to the sacred implications. In any event, it is unlikely that one freshwater source could have provided one million people, which Plato's Atlantis was believed to have.

A counter-conclusion to the idea for there is a chance that the Richat Structure could be Plato's Atlantis is that it's located 400 miles to the inland side and rises 1300 feet above sea level. However, some scholars have suggested that the time period of 12,000 years before the structure may have been very close to ocean level , as long as the ocean's levels were significantly higher towards the end in the Younger Dryas. There is a possibility the possibility of a marine linkage could be in place to connect to the Richat Structure to either the Mediterranean Sea in the north or to the Atlantic Ocean in the west. If it was the case that Richat Structure was in no doubt an island towards the end of Younger Dryas It could be possible that it would be invulnerable to waves. The striations on the sand surrounding the structure provide clear indications of tidal wave activity close to 12,000 years ago.

A French project was shipped off to Mauritania for a few years before filming an account of the structure and conduct major discoveries. Many fascinating revelations were revealed. For starters, clearly the Richat Structure appears to be something extraordinary from the ground. From a distance the seemingly unnoticeable structure resembles another slope. From a distance, the real size and uniqueness in Richat Structure Richat Structure be appreciated. Additionally, several artifacts were discovered that had doubtful source. They included gun balls that were that were intended for ships or oceanic equipment, as well as fishing nets. The antiquities suggest an idea that the Richat Structure might at one time have been located near the water.

It was speculated that the underground geology beneath the Richat Structure could be rising by 1.3 inches every year for the preceding 12,000 years.

years. This theory is based on the assumption the ocean levels did not exist prior to prior to 1300 feet higher in more feet during Younger Dryas; the last time that the Richat Structure would have been submerged or at an adrift level, according to standard earth scientists was a lengthy period prior to that to the time that Homo sapiens had ever speciated.

In 2006, researchers discovered that the continental area of Antarctica increased by 1.6 inches every year. The reason for this was the melting polar icecap reducing the burden on the basic geology, which is causing the land to gradually rise because the ice cap melts due to an overall temperature increase. Another possibility could be that Antarctica's land beneath Antarctica can be lifted via some bradyseismic process, through which the underground action of geography steadily elevates the land's geology via structural movements. This is the same as bradyseism that is negative, in where the earth is gradually being brought down due to structural actions. Because of the Richat Structure, it is unclear whether positive bradyseism would suffice to lift the structure 1300 feet above the ocean over the course of approximately 12,000 years, in spite of the fact that it's definitely in the realm of possibility.

The Richat Structure, otherwise called the Eye of the Sahara is currently located in a cold region that isn't suitable for humanhabitation. In the past, however the Sahara desert and the area that is part that is part of the Richat Structure was a lavish paradise. Numerous huge freshwater lakes were found in across the Sahara Desert, including the massive Lake Maghreb arranged in northern Mauritania and the largest freshwater lake on earth at the time. Could these lakes be the site of an ancient and technologically advanced marine civilization?

There are several significant reasons for the reason that it is possible that the Richat Structure might have been identified with Plato's Atlantis. The circular design of the construction, featuring raised roundabout mounts, separated from dejections that could contain water, suggests Atlantis as imagined by Plato. The combination of positive bradyseismic movements that is seen in cutting-edge Antarctica and ascent of the ocean may be a possible explanation for why the Richat Structure is so much from the ocean's surface in the present. The freshwater spring that is located on the island that is the focal point in the Richat Structure is suggestive of the Poseidon's sanctuary spring. The treasures discovered on the site provide evidence of the presence of humans within the area for more than 10,000 years. There are plausible maritime connections with and the Mediterranean Sea in the north or the

Atlantic Ocean in the south in The Atlantic Ocean in the south during Younger Dryas support the way that the region could be the site of humans who were living in the distant past. In the end, the presence of large lakes close by in the Pleistocene suggests that the region, despite being hostile and without human settlement currently, may have supported an enormous development during earlier periods. Further investigation will prove or demolish this Richat Structure as a potential location in Plato's Atlantis.

It is certainly possible it is possible, but unlikely, that an old-fashioned nautical advance was referred to as"the" Sahara Desert home 15,000 years before. To show this with convincing proof further excavations must be conducted within the Richat Structure. Despite the legitimacy of this scenario it is not possible to prove that this Richat Structure could have been the place for Plato's Atlantis. If all else is equal the structure could be the site of an ancient Atlantis-like marine civilization.

Richat Structure Richat Structure is too remote in actuality from the antiquated Greece and the ancient Egypt to have any cooperation with these civilizations. Both ancient Greece and the antiquated Egypt were founded in the 3000 years BC. Before that the burial of both were during early Stone Age. If they had been the Richat Structure had been the location of Atlantis and Atlantis, it could be the site of an impressive level of progress for around 12,000 years prior to the development in Greece or Egypt. It is unlikely to imagine that the advancements that took place in Greece and Egypt would have preserved records regarding this Richat Structure all through the Stone Age. Only during the Bronze Age, which started at around 3000 BC began, did accounts begin to be established and maintained over long periods of time.

> Athanasius Kircher's Atlantis

Perhaps the most well-known speculation guide to Atlantis was drawn by the map maker Athanasius Kircher Athanasius Kircher, who was a German Jesuit priest who lived in the 17th century. He believed the fact that Atlantis was located beyond to the Strait of Gibraltar on an enormous island in the mid-Atlantic near the Azores. Athanasius Kircher's manual is mentioned with a distinct resemblance to Ignatius the book written by Donnelly in 1882 on his antediluvian world.

Athanasius Kircher was born to the world in Thuringia, Germany in 1602 to the Roman Catholic family. After adolescence that was spent battling Protestant groups in Germany and in constant fear of being caught by them, he was selected in be a member of the Catholic Brotherhood of 1628 when he was the age of 26. His appointment began his journey as a massive traditional scholar and Egyptologist. In the present, Kircher is

Most famous for his maps most well-known for his map making Atlantis as well as his interpretation to Egyptian hieroglyphics.

Illustration 6: Athanasius Kircher.

in the seventeenth century Kircher was seen as the supreme authority in the seventeenth century on Egyptology. This was the reason why, following the revelation that was the Rosetta Stone in the nineteenth century the translations of his work were questioned and his writings fell into offense. In the words of Sir Wallis Budge, the top of the British museum,

"Numerous authors claimed that they had discovered the route to the hieroglyphics. There are many more claimed with a lack of respect that is hard today, and to understand the essence of the text into a cutting-edge language. One of them should be mentioned Athanasius Kircher, who in the seventeenth century declared that he had discovered the route to hieroglyphic engravings. the interpretations he printed on his Oedipus Aegyptiacus were utterly untrue However, since they were developed in a language that was learned, many people of the time believed that they were accurate."

Other researchers, including the Danish Egyptologist the Dr. Erik Iversen, a professor of the University of Copenhagen, took an entirely different view regarding the work of Kircher. According to Iversen

It is the proof of Kircher's authenticity that led him to discover the value of a phonetic Egyptian symbols. From a humanistic as well as a scholarly standpoint Egyptology could be a bit grateful to have Churchr as its founding father."

Despite these mixed reports from scholars, Kircher is today perceived as the ancestor of Egyptology.

Illustration 7: Churchr's guide of Atlantis in the mid-Atlantic region.

Ircher is also famous in his work The Subterranean World which he published in 1664. It is described as a composition of land which is composed of volcanism and traces a portion of the Atlantis turmoil that he believed was caused by volcanic activity. When he was pursuing his research for his work, Kircher broadly had himself taken down by a snag in the Mt. Vesuvius within a short time after a scream to observe the inside actions of a fountain of magma that was liquid. According to Kircher, Atlantis was situated in the mid-Atlantic region, in contrast with the Azores. The guide that Kircher drew attention to in the attention of his work The

Subterranean World appearance Atlantis within this region was replicated in the work of Ignatius the Donnelly of his work The Antediluvian World. It is evident that his understanding of the Plato's Dialogs and his speculation on the location of Atlantis has affected the grant of this subject until the present day. Donnelly himself spoke of the unique ideas of Kircher, creating an idea that portrayed the existence of an Atlantean domain that arose from an midAtlantic home island, delivering states across Africa, Europe and the Americas, Africa, Europe and

India. The most absurd theories for Atlantis

The composition of Atlantis will be complete without a clear and accurate depiction of the restriction of speculations. The most likely restricting scenarios were discussed above to make it clear that Atlantis was located in the southern part of Spain, Mauritania, or the Azores. The next part of this article will look at the most ridiculous speculations regarding the location of Atlantis and the Bimini Road and the city submerged in Cuba, Yonaguni, and Nan Madol.

>"The Bimini Road: A possible alternative to Atlantis located in the Bahamas

North Bimini and South Bimini together comprise the entire area of Bimini, which is the northernmost portion in Bimini, which is the northernmost part of Bahamian archipelago. Together they cover 9 square miles of land area with a population of 1900 residents. North Bimini, the bigger of the two islands is the closest point in the Bahamas to the United States. The name Bimini is a reference to two separate islands, in indigenous Lucayan language.

Islands of Bimini appear in Bahamian mythology. South Bimini island is notable because it is the location for Bimini's Fountain of Youth found by the Spanish traveler Juan Ponce de Leon in the 16th century. North Bimini is the area of the Bimini Road, a 1 1/2 mile long underwater street that is within 20-foot water in the ocean off the island's northwestern coastline. The street was discovered in the year 1968 in the year 1968 by French climber Jacques Mayol.

Since its discovery in 1968 it has been the Bimini Road has been studied by professor

David Zink of Lamar Radiocarbon dating of shells used in the mortar used between limestone asphalt blocks dates the beginning for the Bimini Road in the 1500s BC about 100 years following The Thera ejection. The Bimini Road could have been constructed by Atlantean rebels who fled from the Mediterranean Sea?

The likelihood that Bimini Road Bimini Road has a say in Plato's Atlantis is not certain. Even though that the dating by radiocarbon of the road suggests that the period might be a good fit, Minoan Atlantean Greek exiles might have had to construct a transoceanic junction on warships to travel smaller distances across the Mediterranean in order to reach Bimini. However, regardless of whether expedition was possible in a novel way What would be benefits of going towards the Bahamas? Isn't there a reason to go to Europe or the Azores or even the Azores be better than

were active at University in Texas.

Canary Islands give a similarly suitable asylum, but at a cheaper cost? While appealing however, they are not the most ideal location. Bimini Road stays one of the most unreal locations to build possibly an Atlantean colony.

>> The city that is underwater in Cuba

In 2001 the year 2001, in 2001, a Canadian oceanographic firm was carrying out an undersea study of land on the western bank of Cuba. The firm was contracted by the government agency under Fidel Castro to hunt submerged Spanish fortune vessels off the coast of Cuba. When looking at a two-square-mile area of interest on in the Guanahacabibes Peninsula, which is the westernmost point of Cuba The group that was overseeing the area observed some strange sonar readings. Out of the vast expanses of underwater sand ridgeswas an array of stone structures resembling

The pyramids appear to be forming onto the Sonar Screen. Perhaps this could represent a city submerged?

The ocean's bottom pyramids, which were clearly fake designs created by humans found 2300 feet beneath the ocean floor. Strangely, Homo sapiens wasn't on earth at the time the sea floor was above sea level. There has to be a reason regarding this mystery. As per some experts, the city could have been lowered as a result of an interaction of negative bradyseismic actions as well as rising sea levels. The negative bradyseismic effect is a reference to the lowering of land to lower elevation due to plate tectonics. In any event, for all of this to be plausible considering the historical context of ocean levels over the past hundred millennia The city would have to be around fifty years old. What is the most likely symbol from such a relic on the west coast of Cuba and would this city be able to have any influence in Plato's Atlantis?

Illustration 8 Cuba's submerged city circa. 500.000 BC.

Although this archeological site likely not to be a part of Atlantis because of its fleeting nature and ambiguous spatial context but it offers a fascinating mystery that the future experts will have to solve. One explanation that has been proposed is that a land bridge was once in existence that ran across through the Gulf of Mexico between the western bank of Cuba and the Yucatan Peninsula. The illustration of this land-span is in an Mayan codex dating back to 2000 BC. It is possible that Cuba's submerged city is a sign of the existence of a pre-Mayan advanced civilization in the western part of Cuba prior to the final Ice Age. While the location is certainly fascinating and leaves plenty of questions unanswered, it is more likely than not doesn't have anything to have anything to do with Plato's Atlantis.

>> Nan Madol

Nan Madol, an archeological site located in Micronesia is the most important example of an Atlantis best example of the South Pacific. The city is located within the Hawaiian island Pohnpei which is the capital Island of Micronesia. Federated States of Micronesia. Micronesia is a trust that was previously an area in that of the American Pacific, yet is now a sovereign state in a free and open relations and a free relationship with United States. United States. The

Federated States of Micronesia envelops precisely 600 islands that cover more than 1 million square kilometers in the southern part of the Pacific Ocean. The archipelagic state is situated in a distant part within the Pacific Ocean found 2,000 miles south of Japan 2,200 miles to the north of Australia and two hundred miles to the southwest of Hawaii.

Illustration 9 A view of the island Pohnpei, Micronesia, where Nan Madol was built.

Here are evidence of the humans' home here are evidence of human settlement at Nan Madol going back 2,000 years. Stone tools and evidence of agricultural business in the islands of Pohnpei are believed to date back to the early century AD. Despite the long time of living, the development of the city of stone Nan Madol was not begun until about 1000 AD. The city's development was completed by 1628 AD and by that time it was transformed into an administrative seat of the Saudeler Dynasty, who were the chiefs in the Micronesian domain. In 1874 the destroyed and, to a certain extent, lowered city was discovered by Polish educator Jan Stanislaw Kubary while on an expedition to find antiquities to be used in Hamburg Museum. Hamburg Museum.

Nan Madol filled a double requirement. First Nan Madol was a city that served as the capital city of the Micronesian realm as well as the place of its chief. The head demanded that tribal chiefs of commonplace and their families be based in Nan Madol rather than their island homes. This increased the confidence of the ruler. In addition, when they were viewed as steady by the ruler and separated away from the people they were ruling, tribal leaders were easier to manage and the common sense of unwavering loyalty towards the head with respect to the chief of the tribe was encouraged. Then, Nan Madol's magnificent structures were constructed as burial grounds for former rulers. Much like the pyramids of the past Egypt Nan Madol built to protect the memories of the old sovereigns and to establish the legitimacy of the current administration time.

Nan Madol site Nan Madol site incorporates 6 square miles, and 100 to a certain extent, lower or larger structure made of waterstone. The structures were built on fake islands made of coral. A stone structure protects the site. The primary reason for those dividers of stone was to guard the city from Polynesian and Melanesian intrusions. While Nan Madol was a city Nan Madol was never taken by invaders due to the strong dividers it had however, global temperature changes has caused the structures to slowly retreat beneath the waves.

Illustration 10, James Churchward (1851-1936).

Numerous researchers have linked Nan Madol with the lost city of Atlantis. Educator Bill Ballinger of California States University-Northridge hypothesized that Nan Madol was worked by Greek pilgrims who endure the Thera emission and emigrated toward the South Pacific. Another important knowledge of Nan Madol is that the Nan Madol site was advanced by James Churchward, a British sea engineer and pilgrim known for his invention of the protective plating used on Dreadnought-class warships in World War I. According to Churchward his research, Nan Madol is traceable all the way at least 48,000 BC and is a remnant of the landmass that was lost to Mu the twin civilization that was part of Atlantis. Like Lemuria in

The Indian Ocean, Mu was believed to have extended over all of the Pacific Ocean from Australia to the shores of South America. Churchward believed that antiquated writings discovered in India advised that this area was home to more than 60 million people who participated in a higher level of technological advancement than Britain or America during the 20th century. Additionally, Churchward asserted that the mainland vanished beneath the waves around 12,000 years earlier than the close in the Younger Dryas. This theory is inseparable from the theory the idea that Atlantis as well as Mu was both sinister continents that were submerged by global rise in ocean levels in the Younger Dryas, when a bolide struck the planet's surface on the northern part of the Equator. The bolide's movement generated heat and energy, which then melted north-polar's ice cap which caused the oceans of the world to rise, engulfing Atlantis as well as Mu. Nan Madol, as indicated by this theory was created more than 12,000 years earlier and is a remnant of the lost continent.

Illustration 11. Churchward's missing Landmass Mu.

>> Yonaguni

Yonaguni is the southernmost island in the Japanese archipelago, lies just 67 miles to the north of Taiwan. It is famous in Japanese mythology as being only inhabited by women in the past during events. It covers an area that is 11 sq miles, and the population was around 1700. The islet of Yonaguni is primarily known for its seaward Yonaguni underwater landmark. The monument was discovered on the island in 1986, by Kiharicho Aratake, who was conducting an underwater expedition looking for sharks with hammerheads. Since its discovery it has Yonaguni Monument has been vigorously scrutinized by geologists and archeologists all over the world.

The renowned writer Graham Hancock has intensely investigated the Yonaguni Monument. Hancock suggests the possibility that the Yonaguni Monument might be an example of construction by businessmen that was demolished in the midst of rapid rise of the ocean's level during the late Younger Dryas around 10,000 BC. This is based on the fact that the Yonaguni Monument which is now situated 75 feet deep in the sea floor was last elevated above ocean level in the year 10,000 BC. Due to variations in the ocean's level that followed, the monument was then reduced. It isn't clear if it is true that the Yonaguni Monument has a relationship to the hypothetical lost mainland of Mu isn't known. However, what is certain in any event it is this: the Yonaguni Monument is too remote in existence to have any connection to Plato's Atlantis.

Chapter 7: The Thera Eruption

• The Santorini Caldera today

Santorini is an Cycladic island located in Santorini, a Cycladic island in the south of Aegean Sea that lies around 70 nautical miles to the north of Crete. It is comprised of a circular caldera of marine that measures 8 miles by 4 miles and a surface area in the region of 32 square miles. Within the caldera is an unmistakable island named Nea Kameni, signifying "new devouring island" in Greek. Nea Kameni is a reference to constant volcanism of the island. A few tiny islands of no significance make up on the Santorini archipelago. Presently, Santorini is known for its whitewashed Greek towns built on cliffs overlooking the cove that is brimming with sparkling blue waters. Santorini is the largest and most renowned island that attracts vacationers from The Aegean Sea. It is adorned with cobblestone walkways and craftsmanship exhibits Akrotiri, the main city of the island of Akrotiri is full of sentiment and beauty.

Many travelers do not know that Santorini is a functional source of lava. It lies in the middle in Santorini, which is located in the South Aegean Volcanic Arc which is a dynamic geographical problematic area made up of five volcanoes, namely Methana, Milos, Santorini, Nisyros and Kos. This circular region of dynamic eruptions extends across Athens towards west shorelines of Turkey. The area it is visible located at the centre of the volcanic ark provides the reason for Santorini's risky power. It was, in all likelihood responsible for the most massive eruption of volcanic origin in the written record that was the Thera emission in 1600 BC. It is necessary to look 75,000 years back into the distant past to locate an eruption that was more massive than Santorini's. It was the Toba emission that caused the creation of a hereditary bottleneck which practically eliminated all human life across the globe. Although not as massive as the Toba's, Santorini's ejection was large enough to wipe out the most revolutionary technological advancements that humans could have ever seen up to the time of its creation: Atlantis.

Geology and geology in Santorini along with The Thera Eruption of 1600 BC

The rich history of Satorini is evident in the color of its soil. The soil is highlighted by dark pumice stones , and submerged by red ferruginous stones,

The land cosmetics the land cosmetics Santorini is unique within the Aegean. The reasons behind this exceptionality can be traced back to 150 million years ago, when the four pinnacles that are most notable of Santorini were constructed on the ocean floor of the enormous earlier stages of the Sea of Tethys. When they sank, the African as well as Eurasian plates collided on timescales of geologic history as they did, this Sea of Tethys was continuously blocked by land bridges, creating it into the Mediterranean Sea. The huge impact of the African plates and Eurasian plates created the four pinnacles that had formed in the beginning of Santorini to the top of an outer surface of Mediterranean Sea and shaped the island to the extent that we are concerned in the present.

It is located on a subduction zone in a massive molten area The island of Santorini seemed to be in the midst of volcanic eruptions at some point before it was ever framed. According to the research of Dr. Floyd McCoy, a University of Hawaii teacher of geography, the long-standing existence of Santorini was interspersed with tiny eruptions of volcanic rock that occurred like clockwork. The most powerful of these eruptions occurred in the year 1600 BC. According to Professor McCoy the Theran release was 1.5 times bigger than the Tambora eruption, several times larger that Krakatoa's emission. Krakatoa emissions, as well as several times greater than the Mt. St. Helens, as calculated through the logarithmic (non-straight) index of volcanic explosivity.

Table 2. Volcanic explosivesivity records of major, verifiable eruptions.

The Year of Volcanic Explosivity Index of Volcano Eruption

Thera (Santorini-Atlantis) 1400 BC 7.2 Tambora1815, 7 AD

Krakatoa1883 6 AD

Mt. Saint. Helens,1981. 5 AD

Professor McCoy believes that the stage for the Thera eruption was set 75 years earlier, in 1675 BC at the time that a major earthquake hit Santorini. The quake caused destruction across Atlantis, Crete, and central Greece. The sanctuaries collapsed and homes fell however, life went on as normal. Whatever the case the 1675 BC earthquake caused cracks within the earth's crust which allowed magma to leak out from deep within the shelf to fill the huge underground magma chamber beneath Thera. The magma would then be released in the vicinity of 75 years following the event in the legendary Theran eruption of 1600 BC which destroyed Atlantis without a doubt. The eruption of Santorini occurred in

Four phases.

Ability 3: The phases from the Thera eruption.

Phase

Eruption

Phase 1

eruption

Phase 2

Phase 3

Phase 4

The method by which Atlanteans could have had plenty more time in which to flee had they had the foresight to behave so. The main phase, a plinean explosion comparable to the eruption of Mount. Vesuvius in the year 79 AD included massive puffs of dark smoke that erupted from the apex of the gushing spring lavas, causing the island to be covered in dark debris that could extend up to 30 feet below. The forensic examination clearly exposes this layer of debris on the bluffs in Santorini. Phase 2, which is a Phreatomagmatic eruption that would have resulted in the appearance of magma as well as an expanding volcanic cloud. Lightning could have erupted out of the volcano cloud due to electrostatic release between the invigorated particles, triggering the meteorological characteristic. Stage 3 would have been the pyroclastic stream that destroyed all visible objects when they ran over the surface of the Mediterranean Sea. Stage 4 could have caused the demise of the magma chamber underground and caused a devastating final explosion that

of Description

Plinean

Phreatomagmatic

eruption

Pyroclastic flows

Ignimbrite flows

that the release occurred in stages suggests that the island be crushed.

Illustration 12: Atlanteans endeavor to escape in the event that Thera begins to explode.

Although the lava field will one day prove the worst for Atlantis For a long time, it served as a source of life. Due to the numerous earlier eruptions across the millions of years of the early times The islet of Santorini was submerged in a thick covering of fertile volcanic soil. Plato mentions the fact that in Atlantis the trees sported their natural substances throughout the all year, not just during the spring and the late springtime. This is inferred from an emergency medical clinic Mediterranean climate and to the richness that the volcano soil has to offer.

Just a couple of years prior to the huge ejection in 1600 BC There were signs of the future. The repeated tremors caused damage to the Santorini's stone shrines. Breaks in the dividers of their sacred designs, more often than not, brought fear into the island's inhabitants. Since the beginning of time, the Temple of Poseidon was guarded over the city. Now, it is situated straight above the central point of the liquid magma's fountain's caldera, the ancient temple was probably one of the most important structures to endure the most harrowing aspects of the devastation caused from the underground volcanism.

The gushing lava's power was attributed around 7.2 of 10 points on the volcano's explosivity chart however, a new study suggests that it may have been more volatile than was previously believed. In any case, scientists from the field of volcanology confirm that 50 to 100 cubic kilometers of stone and debris were released

in the air after the lava fountain erupted into the air in 1600 BC in the year 1600 BC, triggering an atomic winter, and creating massive ocean waves that flooded the entire Mediterranean shoreline starting from to the Strait of Gibraltar to the Levant and engulfing the entire Atlantean domain. Within 22 minutes of the eruption massive tidal waves swept over Crete. Crete which was the second-most populous island in the Minoan-Atlantean domain, wiping out the entire eastern part of Crete. The western and central segments of Crete, as well as important archeological sites like Knossos, the Palace of Knossos, were preserved because of the higher altitude.

Illustration 13: Speeding up to 500 mph the wave waves generated by the Thera eruption in the year 1600 BC decreased Atlantean provinces located in the eastern and southern Mediterranean within about an hour and a quarter from the time of eruption.

The explosion of 1600 BC wasn't the moment the magma-filled fountain first released. Before the eruption that completely destroyed the Minoan-Atlantean civilization The fountain of magma liquid had been detonating as was clockwork for centuries. The caldera inward of the fountain of gushing magma rose and fell each time it ejected, altering the topographical layout of the island on various occasions in the geographic timescales of the past. The rise and fall of the caldera inward (the cutting edge of the Bay of Santorini) delivered geological setups that were horde. Every now and then the emission would result in the caldera flooded with seawater. It is as present. At times there was a time when there was a time when the interior Bay of Santorini would contain an island ring. In the beginning of humankind, when Santorini Atlantis was first settled by humans the caldera that was in the inner part consisted of a plain that was level. The vast focal plain, hidden by a plethora of volcanic soil, was what made Santorini-Atlantis attractive for humans to settle throughout the centuries, paving the way for the Thera eruption in 1600 BC.

Radiocarbon is the primary method of determining Thera eruption Thera eruption

Two olive trees set high up on a cliff just near Cape Akrotiri were defoliated and were entangled in the 30-foot thick debris layer that formed during The Thera emission. The trees were discovered and radiocarbon-dated with the help of Professor. Walter Friedrich of

Aarhus University in Denmark. The findings were published in the journal Science. Two olive trees that were lowered in pyroclastic streams near Cape Akrotiri were radiocarbon dated to 1627-1600 BC to within 95% of the probability.

Beyond determining the estimated date range of beyond determining the estimated date range for Thera emission, the current research also allows us to calculate the exact time of the eruption. Professor. Eva Panagiotakopulu of the University of Athens took on an innovative method using creepy crawly chitin determine the radiocarbon date of to the Thera emission. Utilizing the remnants of bugs that were found within a home destroyed by the volcanic eruption of Santorini and Atlantis, Dr. Is still in the air that the radioisotopes found on the insects' chitin shells were could be compared to pre-summer or late spring emission. This clever radiocarbon isotope estimate technique, that was embraced by Prof. Panagiotokopulu and distributed in an article published in 2013 in the journal Naturwissenschaften allows the student of historical studies to determine the conditions that led to the Thera eruption took place.

>> A comparison with the Thera eruption with modern eruptions of similar magnitude

The magnitude and scope of 1600 BC emission from Thera cannot be undervalued. Researchers have revealed that the ejection was estimated to be 7.2 on the volcano's record for explosivity, known as VEI. However what is this implying? What size of an expulsion was it in practical terms? It might be the most efficient method to

image the size and extent of the Thera eruption contrasts the emission against a comparable eruption of volcanic origin in the present. The most straightforward explanation for picture the Thera eruption in modern time is the Tambora emission that occurred in Indonesia that occurred in 1815 and was extensively documented by the current science.

Following the Thera eruption The Mount Tambora release was the 2nd most amazing in recorded human experiences, with an estimated 7.0 on the volcanic explosivity files. This emission, contrary to the Thera eruption, was carefully examined by Dutch researchers who documented the boundaries. It occurred on the 10th of April 1815. It occurred during an "year without an early spring" like the extended atomic winter that was 1-extended that caused crop disappointments across the globe and a frenzied worldwide hunger.

The inhabitants of Tambora Island in Indonesia would have been able to escape prior to the devastating expulsion in 1815. Beginning in 1812, the magma chamber under Tambora began to warm. When the magma field beneath Tambora reached at temperatures of 1500 degrees Fahrenheit , and an adsorption of 70, 000 psi, tremors began and shook the island. Constructions made of wood fell, and small waves wreaked havoc on the coast due to irregular movement of the structure.

The Tambora eruption was responsible for a major natural interruption throughout Indonesia. The ejection covered a large portion in Southeast Asia in a thick pile of volcanic debris and blasts could be heard as far as 1600 miles. Sir Stamford Raffles, the originator of Singapore was located in Indonesia at the time, and witnessed the explosion from a distance

"The primary blasts heard on this island on the evening of 5 April. They were heard in every quarter and continued in a series of blasts until the following day. The sound could be, as a main example, attributed to a distant cannon to the point that a group of soldiers were

The Djocjocarta area was visited by the police with the belief that a nearby post was being attacked and that near the coast, boats were sent to assist in the journey of a boat believed to be in trouble."

- Sir Stamford Raffles' diary The sequela of the Tambora eruption left vast areas of death and destruction throughout The Indonesian archipelago. All human dwellings on Tambora's island Tambora in total destruction which was subsequently lowered by huge streams of pyroclastic. Huge ocean piles of drifting debris, pumice, and debris blocked the transport pathways, which brought exchange to a halt. The following

The atomic winter was responsible for a large number of deaths throughout the globe because of the disappointments of harvest. According to Lieutenant. Philips, a partner of

Sir Stamford Raffles and lieutenant in the Royal Navy, who likewise was a witness to the eruption

from an adjacent island from an island that is adjacent, the eruptions of lava was a terrible: "On my outing towards the western part on the island I made my way through the entirety of Dompo as well as a dazzling part of Bima. The shocking plight to which the inhabitants were reduced is awe-inspiring to see. There was still on and about the last pieces of carcasses, along with the characteristics of where many others were burial sites: towns are all abandoned and the homes shattered with the survivors wandered about looking for food. After the ejection in the past, a severe loose bowels epidemic has swept through Bima, Dompo, and Sang'ir. It has wiped out an astonishing amount of people. The assumption is made by people living there that it was brought to the surface by drinking water that has been contaminated by cinders. Horses are also suffering in large numbers and from a common complaint."

- -- Lieutenant. Philips, Royal Navy The effects on 1815's Mount Tambora emission could be felt from a distances. The actual tuft traveled thirty miles in the upper stratosphere, and was evident from Jakarta. The sound of the ejection was heard all over the world numerous times, and quakes were engulfed throughout in the Pacific Ring of Fire. Worldwide temperatures dropped. The release of poisonous gases in the lower atmosphere, such as sulfuric corrosive carbon monoxide and corrosive rain. This caused the downpour to poisonous crops.

A volcanic eruption that has an VEI greater than Santorini's 7.2 was recorded since the Toba eruption 75,000 years before. The Toba emission was VEI 8. The emission caused a 1000-year nuclear winter, and was responsible to have triggered the final Ice Age. The Toba emission caused a severe population bottleneck for early humans to the point that only 100 set of rearing groups of Homo sapiens remained in the earth's surface following the release. If The Thera eruption of 1660 BC had been larger and had it accelerated to the magnitude of the Toba eruption, it's improbable that any human remains could have survived. In the end, Thera was sufficiently enormous to completely destroy the Minoan-Atlantean area, causing waves as well as massive flooding of the inland regions throughout all of the Mediterranean world. If been the Thera eruption been greater as it actually was it's absurd to think that the ancient Egyptian advancement, or the dated Chinese advancements would have been able to

Have suffered the consequences of the global catastrophic climactic disaster.

Chapter 8: Geography And Temporality

Plato declares that the ancient Atlantis island Atlantis was elliptical and estimated at 3,000 stadia length and 2,000 stadia in width. One stadia in antiquated Greece estimated 606 feet. Based on Plato's representation that the island of Atlantis ought to be at least 340 miles long by at least 230 miles wide. But the gigantic faux expansion in Plato's Atlantis in contrast to the actual Atlantis which is viz. Santorini is caused through a massive error. Greek numbers that were greater than 1000 were written using the type 1 instead of the third zero. For instance, during the time of Plato, the number 3000 would have been composed 300 example 1 , not 3000 as we write it now. This could have led to a miscalculation when translating the real dimensions of the Atlantis island. Atlantis that was perpetuated. If we use a much more sensible 300 stadia length by 200 stadia for the various parts that comprise the entire island, Plato's depiction could reflect a real size of 34 miles long by 23 miles in width. This estimate is true to the exact size and condition of Santorini prior to its 1600 BC eruption.

Plato also reveals the size of Santorini Atlantis the island that was once its focal point, now known as Nea Kameni. It was the home of Poseidon and was estimated to be 5 stadia, or 1/2 mile wide. The number is able to be and firmly believed. In the end, Plato lets us know that a notable mountain was located at a distance of 50 stadia, or 6 miles away from the coast. It is not clear to the mountain Plato was referring, because there are four major mountain tops in Santorini and their form is likely to have changed from the 1600 BC eruption.

Illustration 14: largest island of Atlantis which is where it was that the Temple of Poseidon was developed at a distance of 1/2 mile diameter.

There is no doubt that the understandings of the date as well as the facets of Plato's Atlantis are off by a fraction of 10. In Plato's dialogues, Atlantis was portrayed as "bigger than Libya and Asia Minor". It would seem to imply that Atlantis's island Atlantis must be larger than Santorini by a significant amount. In any event there exists a fundamental explanation to this confusion. In ancient Greek the word that meant greater than was mezon as the word that meant between and between was meson. According to the author's perspective most likely, an error of record was to blame for presenting Atlantis to be "bigger that Libya or Asia Minor" rather than "among Libya and Asia Minor." A quick glance at any map that is a part of that Mediterranean Sea will rapidly uncover that Santorini is located equidistant between Libya as well as Asia Minor, affirming Plato's real significance. What is the significance of Plato's depiction of Atlantis being in existence for over 9000 years prior to the time of Solon? What is the best way to accommodate this with respect to the Thera eruption? Again, a record error is likely to cause a problem. The old-fashioned Greek numeric framework didn't have a need for massive numbers as they did not fit into daily life. The ancient Greeks created the number 900 in the same way as we do today, however they wrote the number 9000 as 900 type 1. We can conclude, in this way that it is highly possible that this could cause confusion. Many people started believing that Atlantis existed for 9000 years before Solon's time. However, it was there for 900 years.

decades before Solon's time.

Chapter 9: Minoan-Atlantean Civilization

>> Discovery

The Minoan human advancement was discovered through the work of British Paleontologist Sir Arthur Evans on the island of Crete following having excavated the Palace of Knossos somewhere in the years 1900 to 1905. Evans suggested that the name Minoan be used to describe the newly discovered progress in spite of the fact that Atlantean was the more compelling and correct choice for the name. The phrase Minoan was first proposed by the German classical scholar Karl Hoeck in his book Minoan Crete. The name of the civilization is derived from the king Minos the name of an apparatus from Greek folklore renowned for his association with Minotaur and the Labyrinth.

Illustration 15 Sir Arthur Evans (1851-1941), the founder of the Atlantean Minoan civilization.

The human development of the Minoan-Atlantean period is divided into four distinct recorded time periods, according to the Greek professor of prehistory, Prof. Nikolaos Platon, the superior historian of the history of ancient Crete. These recorded periods comprise those of the Prepalatial Period, the Protopalacial Period and the Old Palace Period, and the New Palace Period. The creation of the Palace of Knossos, the largest of the Minoan-Atlantean Royal residences dates back back to during the New Palace Period.

Since the discovery in the year 2000, since its discovery, the Minoan Civilization has traced by the current grant up to approximately 2700 BC in the Greek island of Crete as well as three thousand BC located on the island

Santorini. Crete was, long time ago, was thought as the central point in that of the Minoan civilization, but truth is that it was a part with a greater domain. The truth is that the main support for Crete for Minoan civilisation was Santorini which was the capital city in The Atlantean domain. The remains of a mechanically developed early stage of human progress are found in the islands of Santorini that date all the way to 3000 BC. A 5,000 year-old gold figurine of an Ibex was found on Santorini showing that the background to human development on the island was widened significantly further in the past than anyone was able to accept, and that it occurred prior to the onset of both Minoan advancement on Crete and also co-transient with ancient Egypt.

Illustration 16 Ancient Atlantis prior to the Thera emission in 1600 BC.

The mosaics and relics discovered at the shores of Santorini reflect a population that is unparalleled in its richness and diversity in the ancient world. What is the reason why the archeological discoveries on Santorini extraordinary? Santorini was once the capital of a vast domain that stretched across to the Balearic Islands in the west to the Levant in the east. The center of this vast area, Santorini turned into the Manhattan of the Mediterranean Sea, partaking in the riches of a magnitude that was unparalleled until the time of the Roman Empire.

• The Atlantean economy

Santorini could be the main society, with a strong and unified working class. Plato depicts a city that was with free citizens who claimed their residences. There were 60,000 family estates located on Santorini with each one being occupied with its own family members who owned an unrestricted title over the property. The 60, 000 Atlantean families enjoyed an amount of middle class prosperity that was unheard of in the history of the world. The tiny freehold homes were built around Santorini's main plain which was later gone to sea. Many of homes were constructed with delicate dark pumice stones as well as white plaster. They were surrounded by small family farms that were maintained all through the year. The climate of Santorini is said to could sustain agriculture throughout any season, effectively securing the Santorinians from famine.

Law and order was the norm as a necessity in Santorini-Atlantis. It was a remarkably bizarre change in the history of the world the Lord of Atlantis didn't have the authority of life and death over his people. It is interesting to note that the inhabitants from Santorini were seen as residents, not subject. A strict set of laws was enforced on the island, protecting workers from the savage treatment by the elites, and ensuring that Santorini's banking system.

Before it was discovered that Delos served as the depository for The Delian League, Santorini was the most luxurious location within the Mediterranean with the strongest financial system on earth. People who were wealthy from across the Mediterranean were rushing to Santorini to keep silver and gold bullion in the island's bank which gained fame for being the safest and trustworthy on the planet. At the time was the time of the Thera eruption of 1600 BC there was a flood of wealth flowing into Santorini for a long time and it was the most luxurious city in that time period. Bronze Age.

Despite a strong financial structure, Santorini controlled the transportation routes across its Mediterranean Sea. Similar to Venice, Santorini exacted charges on Mediterranean exchanges to support the massive armada of warships. Because warships were the means by which goods were transported throughout the Atlantean region It was considered appropriate that Atlanteans had to take on the burden of the population to assist in with their upkeep and support. Exchange obligations were a part of the strength of the massive Atlantean naval force and also contributed to the harmony of the

Mediterranean. In the Mediterranean, the Atlantean naval force defended the 1400-extended Pax Atlantica between 3000 BC between 3000 BC and 1600 BC.

Orichalcum is a metal amalgam that contained heap uses was another source of Santorini's huge abundance. Santorini-Atlantis had a spectacular business model in

the creation and the use of this composite was used for the building of vessels, equipment and the process of development. Despite being mentioned prominently in Plato's discourses, the precise metallic sythesis for Orichalcum was not known for an extended period of time following the Thera eruption, because the details on the most effective way to create it was lost in the demise of Atlantis.

In 2015 the year 2015, in 2015, an Italian project led by Prof. Sebastiano Tusa, Professor of Archeology at the University of Palermo and Sicily's Commissioner for Archeology, was set to alter the course of events. The excavations discovered 39 orichalcum ingots within an indented kitchen of the Minoan-Atlantean period in the sea's bottom just off the shores of Sicily. The kitchen, which was the only survived the huge tsunamis caused during the 1660 BC eruption, remained its cargo in pristine condition over the years at the bottom of the ocean. Orichalcum's ingots were taken to the surface and studied in Rome by a reputable confirmation firm for metal handling using an X-beam fluorescent. The analysis revealed that the ingots were enriched with 80percent copper and 20 percent zinc, followed by debasements of nickel, lead and gold. The isotopic compositions of the metallic composites found in the ingots were in sync with the known minerals of Santorini. Santorini. The isotopic compositions of these minerals are found nowhere elsewhere within the Mediterranean.

According to Plato orichalcum's value was second only after gold's value in the Minoan Atlantean world. The high worth that is attributed to Atlantean orichalcum during the following thousands of years BC was attributed to its deficiency and utility during its use in the Late Bronze Age. It was the Temple of Poseidon located midway between Santorini and Atlantis, on the location of Nea Kameni, was constructed using silver, gold, and orichalcum. Plato declares that the Poseidon's fortification of Atlantis "streaked in the bright red luminescence from orichalcum". The central point in the sanctuary was enriched with one mainstay of orichalcum , upon which Poseidon's Laws of Poseidon were recorded. The pinkish tinge in Atlantean orichalcum was attributed to the part of the minerals that were found on Santorini. Phreatomagmatic emission back to back on the island during the course of centuries had mixed the soil of Santorini-Atlantis and ferruginous iron oxides and gave the orichalcum found with a beautiful rosy shade.

Pliny The Elder who wrote in the 1st century AD wrote that orichalcum even though it was abundant in ounces, wasn't used for a very long time due to the fact that "the mines were exhausted." He was to a certain extent right. The reason for the loss of the world's supply of orichalcum is the Santorini-Atlantis island was completely destroyed in the year 1600 BC. It was the primary location in the world that had the information needed to make orichalcum.

In addition, Santorini Atlantis was the most important place in the world with regularly occurring rocks that contain an exact recipe of ferruginous oxides as well as the phreatomagmatic minerals that are expected to provide orichalcum in a large amount.

Perhaps there is no other place within the well-studied areas of the globe where people by abundance is more tranquil than Santorini. Santorini. It wasn't just that Santorini was the seat of power in the Atlantean realm and the seat of the ruler, but it was also the residence of a powerful and serene working class that put a lot of money into their island. In contrast to Egypt where slaves who worked in impoverished conditions could ascend and kill their masters at any moment the booze and glitz of class was the norm in Santorini. The top class shopped in the same open-air markets similar to the Santorinian working class. Robbery and minor wrongdoing was nearly unfathomable. Santorinian residents were proud of their the island's home and welcomed the finest and brightest across the Mediterranean to join them.

Orn Santorini is hardly akin to the ancient capital that was the capital of Santorini is a far cry from the old capital of Atlantean domain, except perhaps because of it's circular inner Tidal Pond. If one has some imagination and contrast with the Thera caldera with the works of Plato and works, it is possible to see how dated Atlantis might have appeared. This caldera that is which is currently covered by water, used to be the region which was once the center of Atlantis as described by Plato. The focal fields were surrounded by fertile volcanic soils derived due to repeated Theran emission that ran north for million of years. There was no place on earth that could boast such abundant soil or amazing climate conditions as Santorini. Santorini.

It's a reasonable assessment to state it was Atlantis was one of the enjoyable and extravagant place in the universe for lengthy periods in the history of mankind's series of adventures. People and rulers of Atlantis could have no doubt endorsed this view of their realm. If they had agreed however, perhaps it was more prudent to the Atlanteans to pay attention to the words of the man who was the reason their memories would have been lost"Let no one nor any realm remain content until the end. Solon's warning about pride's dangers is heard across the sands of arid deserts of the past.

• Greco-Atlantean culture: It is the Cult of Poseidon

The gods of ancient Greece and the gods of Atlantis were in essence identical. However, in light of the information provided by the gods to our time, we can see that the pantheons of deity from Greece as well as Atlantis are quite similar. As an example, for instance, ancestor and patron lord of Atlantis was thought to be Poseidon who was the Greek god of the sea.

Poseidon was so loved by the people of Atlantis so much that the largest and most recognizable and important structure of the Atlantis city is a massive sanctuary complex dedicated to Poseidon. The way Greece and Athens were both devoted to the same gods evidently proves that they are from the same social tradition.

The primary function of oseidon in Atlantis is best explained through the role of the ocean within The Minoan economy. Incredibly, the power of the sea was the most powerful in the Mediterranean prior to the Thera expulsion Minoans established an arrangement of shipping lanes that stretched across the Levant towards Spain. The shipping lanes were backed by warships, the infamous boats that were used in traditional Greek antiquity.

• "The Stone of Atlantis

Plato states that Atlantean development was largely dependent on three major varieties in stone: white marl dark pumice and red stone. White marble was used in the Greeks as well as the Atlanteans to create amazing sculptures of creatures and people that were renowned for their authenticity, even after the rise in the Roman Empire. The Atlanteans employed white marble to create the statues of their gods, goddesses and beings, like the massive statue of Poseidon that was erected in the city's central sanctuary. The Atlanteans also used dark pumice, as portrayed by Plato. The fact that Atlantis was built upon a functional volcanic area meant that dark pumice was always easy to find. Pumice is light and could be found close to Atlantis to be used for development projects. This meant that it could be easily loaded onto barges and transported by waterway starting at one end of the island and moving to the next to be used in building structures. The dark pumice was the most affordable stone found in Atlantis and was commonly used to construct private houses and open-air markets. In addition, red rock was also utilized in Atlantis to build constructions and sculptures.

--"The Seven Atlantean Frescoes of Akrotiri

The seven frescoes found in Akrotiri are important because they offer the sophisticated onlooker unparalleled insight into the everyday life and daily life of Atlanteans. Beginning in 1967, excavations by the Greek classicalist the Greek classicist Dr. Nicholas Marinatos have uncovered many frescoes from Atlantis that survived the Theran expulsion. The frescoes can be found throughout homes that range from those of the poor to the houses of the wealthy. The Atlanteans employed a unique combination of mineral-based paints as well as natural fixatives to create the

frescoes. The intricate and vibrant work incorporates the colors of red, blue, purple pink, saffron, and blue. The frescoes are believed to highlight the Atlanteans fascination in the everyday and deep world. As per Dr. Marinatos,

"a piece of art that was a by the custom that was understandable and surprising. The idea is that craftsmanship was a reflection of the positive aspects of the public which the person who was watching was part. Therefore, the relationship between watchers and craftsmanship was tight and the potential of the canvas was important...the subjects were based on strictly interactions, though these might be as straightforward. Political resemblance is in all likelihood absent."

The focus on the topics of the otherworldly and creature indicates that the outdated Atlanteans weren't a shallow group. The Atlanteans acknowledged a deeper significance to the world beyond the realms of the mundane and physical. This is evident in their divider and specialty frescoes dating to the 1800s BC.

The most significant of Atltantean frescoes is without doubt The Marine Fresco. It is the Marine Fresco is perhaps the most important representation that is still in existence of Atlantis. The fresco depicts Atlantis in its most likely state towards the 1800 BC. The viewer is placed between the main island of Atlantis and viz. Nea Kameni, and the end of the volcano in which other tiny structures appear to line the upper layer of steep slopes similar to the advanced Santorini. The city that is the focal point of Atlantis depicted in the fresco is shown that it is populated heavily and covered by a huge channel that separates Nea Kameni from the caldera's edge. From the viewpoint shown on the painting, the viewer cannot see the interlocking configuration of channels which could have existed further farther inland in Nea Kameni as depicted in Plato.

Illustration 17 Atlantean ships, part of the Marine Fresco.

The parts that comprise the Marine Fresco are additionally slanted. The painting depicts the group of Atlantean naval forces that are moving towards the focal island Nea Kameni. The vessels appear, according to all indications, to have been controlled by rowers and not sails, which is consistent with the way it was believed that Atlantean warships were designed to be used.

Mediterranean Sea and travel within the

They weren't designed to be used overseas.

voyages, as a variety of researchers have proposed. This style Marine Fresco is more likened to impressionism rather than authentic. For instance, the Atlantean head of the naval operation's chief for instance, is depicted as being larger that the actual island Nea Kameni in itself. This indicates that the features suggested by the paintings included in the Marine Fresco don't mirror the real elements of Atlantis. The second largest painting of the entire collection is known as The Papyrus Fresco. It is the Papyrus Fresco shows a gathering of three papyrus plants that had grown to the size of the magma stream that runs through Atlantis. That Atlanteans brought papyrus plant species from Egypt is evidence of an important amount of trade between Atlantis as well as Egypt. Egypt was at the same time an element of the Atlantean area. The fresco further suggests that the Atlanteans employed Egyptian papyrus paper to make their books as well as original copies. There could be fragments of Atlantean papyrus with a holdback the papyrus that is found on Akrotiri from the time of the discovery to the present day? It's a bit unlikely given the sheer heat and energy emitted through the eruption of the volcano in the year 1600 BC that destroyed the city. In all likelihood, in the event that an original copy or two were encased in the glass container or container, and then immediately covered with pumice, it isn't hard to imagine that some fragments of Atlantean paper could be present, waiting the possibility of being discovered.

another significant fresco that was discovered within Atlantis was the Monkey Fresco. This Monkey Fresco shows a company comprising no less than six monkeys soaring up a stone slope in order to escape from two dogs. Monkeys were seen as an oath-like creature in the past of Atlantis. They were frequently depicted as gatekeepers for consecrated designated areas, and also as the inhabitants of Atlantean sanctuary. The reasons behind why Atlanteans were awed by monkeys and sheltered their animals in their sanctuary is unclear. The only thing that is certain regardless is that the old world primate species, beginning in Africa were found on

Atlantis at the time of ancient times A fossilized skull of a primate was discovered on Santorini in 1983.

Lady Fresco Lady Fresco is significant in due to the fact that it reflects the most cutting-edge audience with regards to the Minoan-Atlantean fashion of dressing. The fresco depicts a classy woman being attired by her servants. The model is dressed in cosmetics as well as a beautiful flowing dress , with a typical Minoan coat that reveals her bosoms. In the past of Atlantis this is what it appears to be women's clothing was often exposed their bosoms to general public view. The reasons for this are unclear but it does not appear to be the case in central Greece. Whatever the reason, this clothes were considered to be appropriate for a socially acceptable dress in Atlantis.

Illustration 18 Seven frescoes from Akrotiri depict the daily life of Akrotiri could have been like in the time of Atlanteans.

The Fisherman Fresco depicts a child carrying a fish in a formal proposal for the temple of Poseidon. Fish was used as a means of offering a vote to the Poseidon's ministers sanctuary. Fish's use as a means of proposing a vote to the city's god of benefaction is a clear indication of the importance of fish as a symbol of the elites from Atlantis. The evidence suggests that Atlantis was a bit dependent on fish for the care of its population of 1 million. It is based on the idea that, although it was a very productive was the land available in the plain that was the focal point of Atlantis wasn't sufficient to produce enough food supplies to feed Atlantis the vast population that was cultivated using old-fashioned cultivation techniques. It was estimated that the Atlanteans depended heavily on Egypt and the Egyptian states for imports of food in all

Keep up with the population density that is Santorini. Egypt also profited from this trade via its use in an Atlantean dealer armada to transport its goods to the market.

Chapter 10: Submerged Colonies

The next part will deal with the four important Atlantean states that are currently in the Mediterranean Sea. The states included: 1.) Baiae in Italyeraclion in Egypt

2.) Atlit-Yam in Israel

3.) Pavlopetri in GreeceThese four important frontier settlements of Atlantis were reduced in 1600 BC due to the tsunami that was that was caused through The Thera emission. The spread of Minoan Atlantean settlements across Italy up to Levant illustrates the vast geographical scope of the Minoan-Atlantean world at its peak in the second millennium BC prior to the eruption. An archeological investigation at the Atlantean states that lie along the Mediterranean shoreline has revealed amazing insight into the ways of life, work and the religion and religion of SantoriniAtlantis itself. Relics that have been found in these secured undersea areas are a burden for us to take an in-depth look at the history of the Atlanteans particularly considering that many of the rare items that likely existed on Santorini were destroyed by the Thera eruption, making the relics in a way that was unobservable to modern science.

>> I. Baiae

Four thousand years before that time, the Minoan-Atlantean realm encompassed the entire western shore of Italy stretching to Etruria towards the northern part of the country, and the Sicilian Strait in the south. Its western coastline of Italy was covered with several Atlantean states. These states set the foundations to support the Etruscan human development that was the mainstay of the ancient Rome. The most important part from the Western Italian riviera during Atlantean times was Baiae, the port city. Baiae. Baiae is currently located beneath the sea located in the Bay of Naples and a popular destination for divers, was an thriving Atlantean city, which was authenticated around the third millennium years BC. The city was home to an estimated area of 150,000 inhabitants, Baiae was the territorial capital of the Atlantean region of Italy and was an important local spot for legislative and business matters. It is, however, Baiae is one of the most buzzing cities in the old world, Baiae was the Thera removal of

1600 BC led to the sinking of the city in the year 1600 BC. The remains of the undersea city of Baiae are from the second millennium BC and were submerged due to the torrents that were accelerated during the 1660 BC Thera volcano.

The Thera fountain of magma liquid ejected huge waves filled with pumice and debris from pyroclastic streams swept through the Mediterranean Sea every which way. The moment the stream, estimated at 200 feet tall reached the Straits of Sicily and sank into the sea, the channeling of the geography caused due to the thinness of the Straits caused the waves to rise substantially higher, reaching more than 600 feet in height. This massive wave broke out of at the Straits of Sicily into the Tyrhennian Sea going at velocities of 500 miles per hour, striking the Italian coast , and never stopping to lower Baiae beneath the waves.

Due to the delicate nature that is the Baiaen soil it was not possible for the tidal waves to simply travel in the inland direction and then it would return into the ocean for within a couple of days following the fact. In all likelihood the tidal waves caused the liquefaction and swell of the soil, and Baiae was formed. This led to the collapse of several significant structures like Baiae, which was the Atlantean refuge in Poseidon located in Baiae. The sanctuary was built around the coastline and was extremely ineffective against the rough oceans created by the eruption of volcanic ash.

It is believed that the Roman Antiquarian Plutarch was famous for his account of the violent floods of the ancient Rome. The specialist in history describes the massive floods that occurred during which the Tiber River was able to conquer its banks. Plutarch may have been alluded to the tidal waves that occurred during the Thera ejection in 1600 BC that were advancing along to the Tiber River. It is possible that the 1600 BC wave that lowered Baiae may also have advanced toward the north , and influenced Rome that at that time was an inactive fishing city. The Torrent waves swept across the Tiber River for miles further inland, submerging the flood plain of Campus Martius. The flooding didn't stop for quite a long time. The students of history know that saltwater was left within the soil for an extremely long time, devouring crops and contaminating soil by releasing salinity.

Based on the origins and remains of submerged remains It is clear that Baiae was constructed by the Atlanteans in the second millennium years BC. Furthermore, these structures were clearly weakened due to the activities of the sea's torrents, and not due to bradyseismic motion which is what has been proven. The level of complexity displayed by the underwater remnants of Baiae offer a short insight into the life in those who lived in the Atlantean civilization. Many of the underwater sculptures served as inspiration for later fine art that were developed in Greece, Rome, and Italy during the Renaissance. Perhaps the most important and well-known among these older Atlantean statues are that of Venus from Baiae.

The discovery that Baiae, the Atlantean Venus from Baiae is believed to be the work of Sir Thomas Hope, a prominent Anglo-Dutch classicalist, savant and interior decorator. Trust was introduced to our world during 1769, in the Netherlands and was the son of the recognizable trader Jan Hope. The father imparted to the child artwork and a fascination with the art and the culture of ancient Greece as well as Rome. However, Jan Hope died abruptly in the Hague at the age of Thomas was only 15 years old of age. In a state of anxiety, Thomas embarked on the Grand Tour of Italy and Greece with his mother and aunties. It was a Grand Tour additionally stirred up his love of art that date back to the ancient times in Greek as well as Roman civilization.

Illustration 19 Sir Thomas Hope, who found the Minoan-Atlantean goddess of Baiae in the bottom of the ocean near the shore of Italy in 1803.

As the heir to an enormous fortune in money, Hope utilized his abundance to finance archeological projects across Italy. One of those efforts was in Baiae during 1802. The campaign of Trust to Baiae was prompted by tales of a vast submerged city stuffed with antique models that were kept in stunning condition that was flawless. Unable to resist the lure, Hope subsidized a submerged archeological project to Baiae to study the shocking facts. Trust's venture was the primary archeological venture planned to discover treasures under the sea rather than on land. He enlisted a group of pearl jumping enthusiasts to explore the bottom of the ocean in search of artifacts. In just a couple of days, archeological discoveries began to accumulate the stunning mosaic floor with a design in an Atlantean style, numerous submerged sculptures that resembled the Greco-Atlantean gods. And, especially that of the Venus Baiae. Baiae.

The revelations provided by Hope offer a short insight into the Hellenic civilization of the old Atlanteans. One of the most important of the undersea discoveries made by Hope were his discovery of the Venus of Baiae, which was discovered from the ocean floor in the year 1803. The artifact, secured by layers of a delicate clay for over 3000 years, was maintained the best of condition on the ocean floor. Trust found the sculpture in an undersea mudbank , and then carried it up to the surface using an amazing system of pulleys and ropes. Through this method the sculpture was carried to London where he displayed it in his antiquities shop.

Illustration 20 Illustration 20: Venus of Baiae.

It is believed that the Venus of Baiae was the principal archeological discovery of Hope's campaign for a long duration. The first thing to note is that evidence is it is possible that Venus of Baiae was etched on the island of Santorini about 4,000 years ago by an Atlantean stoneworker called Cleomenes and spread the word about one of the longest-running Atlantean sculptures used for scientific research. The study into the marble where it was carved by the Venus of Baiae was etched is a reflection of an organization that coordinated the other well-known Atlantean sculptures found on Santorini. Santorini. This kind of organization made up of white marble is present in no other place on the earth. In addition Baiae's Venus of Baiae represents the extent of creative refinement that occurred during the peak of the

Atlantean advancement during the second millennium BC. The level of imagination and authenticity achieved through The Venus of Baiae will remain unsurpassed for a long time following the 1600 BC catastrophe. Thirdly The Venus of Baiae is significant because of the fact that it spawned several of the subsequent masterpieces, including that of

Venus de Medici, presently considered to be the head depiction of the Venusian theme.

The Venus de Medici, an exact reproduction that is a faithful representation of Atlantean Venus of Baiae, is one of the most renowned sculptures of the western development. The sculpture was created by an obscure artist during the first century BC The statue is currently located within the Uffizi Gallery in Rome. It was purchased from the Medici family and was displayed within the Villa Medici in Rome in 1638 or so at the time it was included in the Villa Medici collection by the French artist Francois Perrier. In this way, it was sold across Rome to Florence because the Pope Innocent believed it energised "vulgar behaviour".

The Venus is one of the most copied European sculptures. Louis XIV appointed no under five reproductions of the design for his castles. A more famous copy that was recently acquired by the count of Habuval and called Aphrodite which is located within the Metropolitan Museum of Art in New York City. These replicas can be traced through to the very first Atlantean Venus of Baiae, which was created precisely four thousand years before to an island called Santorini by Cleomenes who was a native of Atlantis.

>> II. Heraclion

It was an excellent idea that helped speed up the discovery of Heraclion which was the Atlanteans vital state of Egypt. It was the work of Dr. Franck Goddio, a excellent French mathematician who spent most of his adult life demonstrating mathematics in the University of Paris. But he was adored by his students and respected by his colleagues,

With his colleagues, Professor Goddio wanted to do something that could be remembered through the years. Was there anything more significant, threatening and important than the revealing of the ancient city of Heraclion? Heraclion is the largest Minoan-Atlantean city along the south Mediterranean coast, has been documented by Egyptian documents dating back to at least the second millennium BC. The problem was that nobody was aware of its precise location. According to antiquated antiquarians and analists, Heraclion was arranged in the northern part of Egypt on the Canopian portion of the Nile. Guidebooks of earlier Ptolemaic

Administration of Egypt illustrate the Canopian portion of the Nile flowing to Aboukir Bay. The narrows were massive, with an estimated the area to be 230 square miles. It is likely that the nature of Aboukir Bay isn't able to be explored in the span of a single man's life.

Illustration 21 Ancient Heraclion, before 1600 BC deluge.

However, professor Goddio. Goddio was no standard man. He. Goddio concocted a clever method of studying the bottom of the ocean in Aboukir Bay by using an amazing sonar instrument that he employed without any prior preparation. The sonar instrument could be pulled from behind a boat , and utilized to look over the sea's base for any anomalies that could be a sign of huge growth. In reality, even using this amazing new technology the survey of Aboukir Bay will in any scenario require a long time to complete. Goddio, Dr. Goddio spread out a guide using probability hypothesis, range, and longitude to ensure that the top

of the inlet was of the inlet in a systematic and reproducible manner. Finally, after an extensive amount of searching of the inlet, of the inlet. Goddio's team struck gold in of 2000. The sonars discovered a massive pillar in the lower portion of Aboukir Bay. It was the very first of many like discoveries.

The discovery will provide an entirely new understanding of the human race's understanding regarding this Atlantean occupation of southern Mediterranean. Stone tablets with engravings from the lower portion of the inlet indicated that Egypt was a client condition that was part of Atlantean origins. Atlantean realm, and not simply enslaved by her. Egyptian hieroglyphics were believed to be combined together with Atlantean sculptures and the fine arts. The evidence found at Heraclion revealed two important facts concerning the place. The first is that Heraclion is an Atlantean city with a significant amount of phonetic and social trade with more notable Egypt. In the second, Heraclion was degraded in the 1600 BC through a mix of ground subsidence and flooding which was probably caused through the same 1660 BC Thera release that decimated Santorini.

The destruction of Heraclion is explained by Heraclion's Tempest Stele, an old Egyptian depiction of the Thera Ejection, engraved on an ancient column found within the Temple of Karnak. The stele was discovered by French classicalist Claude Vandersleyen in 1967 and is believed to date to about 1590 BC 10 years following the flood. The stele depicts an important flood that struck ancient Egypt inundating cities like Heraclion in the same way as other urban communities across northern Egypt. The stele was approved to be erected by Pharaoh Ahmose I to celebrate the epic flood. It was discovered during 2014 by the researcher the researcher Dr. Robert Ritner in the Journal of Near Eastern Studies. According to the stele:

The divine beings brought about the sky appears in the form of a downpour that rages with a dimness in the state of the West and the sky was constantly in a state of chaos and louder than the cries of the majority, and the downpour cried out to the mountains with more force than the underground source of the Nile which is situated in Elephantine."

Egyptologists have argued that the stele depicts delayed effects of the Thera eruption and the flood that it brought across northern Egypt under the reign under the reign of Pharaoh Ahmose I. Based on the representation given in the stele clearly the debris mists emitted through the lava well (starting towards the west of Santorini as depicted in the stele) also triggered precipitation. The precipitation could have created an additional impact of the substance beyond the actual stream, destroying the floods that afflicted northern Egypt.

>> III. Atlit-Yam

In the colder season of year 1984 the in 1984, Dr. Ehud Galili was scuba diving into the distinctive waters of the shoreline from Haifa, Israel. The Dr. Galili, a cultivated jumper and paleologist was taking part in the beautiful underwater scenery that was Haifa Bay. The scene was serene; anemones had a profound effect on the ocean the bottom and clownfish swam throughout their coral hideouts. When the Dr. Galili swam through the reasonably Mediterranean waters, something massive was revealed. Three massive dark columns could be evident rising out of the sand. They were late exposed by undersea flows during the colder season of the year, which were pounding the Haifa shoreline just half a month before. At present, the unfavorable design for three columns of stone could be clearly visible through the murk.

The Dr. Galili, an educator of antiquarianism at the University of Haifa, went further to study. Dr. Galili's lengthy time spent preparing and scouring the world for clues of human settlement made him aware that this was not your typical stone arrangement. The columns of stone were carefully cut and laid out with mathematical precision. A chill ran through the Dr. Galili's back. He could tell the magnitude of the finding.

one month in the aftermath one month after the fact, half a month later. Galili collected a group of archeologists from submerged areas to aid in the underwater excavation. It was too big of a job for one person. The multidisciplinary team provided boats and enormous air hoses that were used to scrub away the sand covering the three columns of stone. The air hoses allowed for the sand cleaned off delicately, without causing harm to the columns themselves. The air hoses blow out the sand was obvious that the size and dimensions of columns was a lot superior than originally believed. In the end, the tops of three columns were rising out of under the sand at the time they first became visible. When the columns were uncovered and inspected, it was clear that they were many times taller than when they first appeared. In addition, they were flanked by several additional columns, each measuring over 10 feet high.

It was said that Dr. Galili had found an Israeli stonehenge. Israel's stonehenge, described in the scholarly writings as Atlit-Yam, could have been atop an elevated precipice, ignoring Haifa Bay during the times of the Atlantean domain prior to the Thera emission in 1600 BC. What then happens was it that Atlit-Yam disappear beneath the waves? Further excavations at the Atlit-Yam location will reveal clues to the way that the massive stone structure was submerged. There is evidence that waves caused damage throughout the Atlit-Yam site that goes all the way to the year 1600 BC which was the time that was the time of Thera emission. This suggests that human habitation is a factor.

Atlit-Yam lasted to the year 1600 BC until it was abruptly eliminated by a massive catastrophe on the seas.

There is evidence that Haifa Bay's Stonehenge was an altar to God. The monoliths of stone that comprise the stonehenge are arranged in a circular arrangement and, in the past it was possible that they had the roof of a domed structure with an oculus in the top. The oculus served as the conductor through which light could flood inside the structure at the time of the solstice at mid-year. The intense light coming through the oculus could have lit the inner safe-haven. Contrary to England's stonehenge Atlit-Yam's circular column could have been the remnants of a much larger structure, which was present at the site in the second millennium BC prior to being destroyed through Thera tsunami. Thera tsunami.

The orientation of the structure towards the solstice of late spring suggests that the reason for its construction was to worship Zeus-Amun, the Greco-Egyptian god who was the sun god , and also the god-of-all-things ruler of all divine beings. Zeus-Amun's central location at the time of the town Atlit-Yam could have increased his significance throughout the Levant. Zeus-Amun, unlike various gods from the old Egyptian pantheon is not simply believed to be a god of the sun He was also once more revered as a sole supernatural god, who was adamant about the denial of any other Egyptian gods.

The love affair between Zeus-Amun and Zeus in ancient Egypt as well as the Levant The two major locations that comprised the Atlantean realm in the second millennium BC illustrates the fact that not every Atlanteans had a polytheistic belief system. There was, in fact, large proportion of people of the Atlantean realm who adhered to a monotheistic beliefs at the time. It is believed that the most likely possible source for their belief was Zeus-Amun , rather than Poseidon since there is no evidence that Poseidon was ever considered a singular god at any time in the Atlantean settlements. Based on the available evidence regarding the monotheistic worship of Zeus-Amun, it is possible to conclude that monotheism was not a secret in ancient Egypt regardless of having been clearly considered to be a minority belief.

>> IV. Pavlopetri

In 1670, four British mariners were swept away from the Island of Elafonisos located in the Gulf of Laconia by a turbulent tempest. One of them were Reverend Elijah Covel, a pastor of the Church of England. Journals of Rev. Covel is in good order and is kept at the University of Cambridge library. The journal mentions that mariners discovered the remains of an earlier ship.

the city was submerged for a long time while searching for fresh water. The city was built under 8 feet of crystal clear blue water that flowed through the waters that separated Elafonisos Island from the mainland.

Rumors of an underwater city located in the Gulf of Laconia have coursed through Greece for a long time. Inspired by these little bits of gossip, and confirmed by Rev. Covel's journal page in 1670, British excavating expert Dr. Nicholas Fleming, a teacher at the University of Cambridge, started an expedition in across the Gulf of Laconia in 1968 to find the missing remains. The teacher traveled into Greece in the spring of 1968 to conduct an expedition close to Elafonisos which was the island on which Reverend Covel was found dead 300 years before. The island, as described by

Greek sources was the only remaining part of the once-incredible Atlantean town of Pavlopetri. After his arrival in Elafonisos the professor Fleming correctly rediscovered the low ruin of Pavlopetri which earned him the honor of being included in the encyclopedias that are published by The University of Cambridge among the few researchers who were fortunate enough to have discovered a forgotten city in the world of antiquity.

As like Dr. Goddio who found Heraclion and the Dr. Fleming created novel surveillance methods to examine the bottom of the ocean in Pavlopetri according to a custom-designed approach for the extraordinary environment of Gulf of Laconia. The Dr. Fleming utilized a sonar cluster dubbed"the Konigsberg Array fit for checking and analyzing the bottom of the ocean with a speed of 750,000 cycles per minute. The sonar structure developed by Dr. Fleming effectively planned the complete metro plan of Pavlopetri in a bid to be to pinpoint the smallest ocean imp in just 8 days. After the sonographic process was completed the Dr. Fleming had gathered 1.4 Terabytes of data on the city's design.

The submerged city of Pavlopetri, Greece has been recorded as being 3000 years old BC from archaeologists. The city, which is located in the Gulf of Laconia close to SantoriniAtlantis and has been reduced from the Thera emission in 1600 BC. Before the ejection Pavlopetri was known as "the rock that is St. Paul" in Greek was a bustling Atlantean city of around a one hundred thousand inhabitants.

Pavlopetri's leaning toward a position along its position in the Gulf of Laconia and nearness to Santorini and Atlantis made it an important exchange location between Atlantis and central Greece. Archeological digs have exposed vast dockyards in which goods such as orichalcum was sunk by warships and placed in stockrooms to be used to be distributed throughout central Greece. It could be argued, therefore it is possible that Pavlopetri was the principal exchange middle point that linked with the capital city SantoriniAtlantis with its central Greek provinces.

Chapter 11: The Bible Is Based On Evidence.

Chronology

The original method of dating we suggest begins with the presumed date of birth of Noah and we provide it as 1660 BC based on the fact that the Bible implies that Noah was an older person at the time it came to the Great Flood. Additionally, Noah had a few hitched children that accompanied Noah on the ark. This lends evidence that he was older enough to have developed, married to posterity by the time that the Flood occurred.

To determine the time for the Great Flood, which we compare to the 200-foot high waves generated from Thera ejection. Thera ejection, an approximate year of about 1600 BC could be given based upon the dating by radiocarbon of peace offerings made by Friedrich and others (1627-1600 BC to inside a 95% probability range). Then we would be able to use the family histories that are contained within the Masoretic Text isolating Noah and Abraham by

Ages 0 to create a plausible sequence that is consistent with the most significant patriarch's approximate birthday.

To foster this request, we require three dates. The first one refers to the time of the Deluge that we can inexactly date at 1600 BC using Radiocarbon dates of The Thera emission. Another date that needs to be considered is the birth date of Noah. We estimate that he was 60 years old age at the time Noah was born. Great Deluge dependent on the manner in which he developed the wedded children who joined Noah in the Ark. His son, Arphaxad, was the first Noah's son to enter the world following the flood. The 3rd important date that we must know is the birth date of Moses. Based on these three dates, we are able to understand the entire scriptural sequence an conceivable manner that is able to be reliant to archeological as well as narrative proof.

The approximate date of Abraham's birth Abraham has been clarified by Egyptian historian Ahmed Osman in his 1987 book Stranger in the Valley of the Kings. According to archeological evidence presented in the book by Osman Abraham's remarkable grandson Joseph was the maternal grandfather of the Egyptian Pharaoh Akhenaten who was the organiser of Egyptian monotheism. He ruled between 1350 and 1335 BC. This important revelation by Osman helps in establishing the scriptural order even more.

To determine the date of the history of Moses and his followers, we turn to the Roman historian Tacitus who offers us an objective and fair account regarding his account of the Jewish Exodus from old Egypt under the administration by the Egyptian pharaoh Bocchoris who reigned between 722 and 715 BC. According to Tacitus,

Many journalists agree that once a disease, that horribly altered the body, erupted over Egypt and the king Bocchoris in search of solutions, sought advice from his prophet Hammon and was urged to cleanse his kingdom and then to move on to another unknown country where this race was is feared by God's beings. People who were at a gathering after a gruelling hunts, and were observing that they would be in the desert, sat mostly in a state of despair, until an exiled person, Moses by name, warned them against looking for relief through God or from man. snubbed by both. They were to instead trust in themselves, and taking as their their idealistic, sent-inspiring pioneer man would first assist them in getting rid of their despair. They agreed with him, and began to wander aimlessly. However, nothing frightened them as much as the lack of water. They were sinking ready to perish in every direction over the plain. Then an entire group of wild horses was said to be withdrawn from their field towards a stone that was hidden by trees. Moses was with them and, guided by the appearance of a green area, discovered a plentiful source of water. This was equipped to Moses with help. After an endless journey for six days and seven nights, they were able to take over an entire country, and from where they drove out the occupants and then built a city and the temple.

-Tacitus, Histories, 5.3 Tacitus, Histories, 5.3 Tacitus affirms that Moses was the one who coordinated the Exodus during the reign of the pharaoh, Bocchoris. In addition the fact that the Bible informs us that Moses was about 80 years old of age when he was announcing the timing that he led the Exodus. No matter if we believe in the exact time of

Moses mentioned in the Bible it is easy to assume that he was a senior citizen when he was announcing the Exodus. So, to be straightforward it is clear that Moses was introduced to the world at around 800 BC.

Tacitus offers the most precise, clear, and reliable account about his account of the Hebrew Exodus from old Egypt at any time written. The author believes that the creator that we must trust Tacitus in his depiction of the event because of his objectiveness and clarity. Furthermore, the author is of the opinion that Ipuwer Papyrus is too obscure to allow the researcher of scriptural studies to get any kind of consensus.

decisions regarding its validity. What is the reason why the scribe's chronologist take any note of the uncertain Ipuwer Papyrus when the record of Tacitus offers an imagined worth representation of the Exodus which cannot be disproved?

As we now know the birth date of Moses and the birth date of Noah We can go all the way back to Masoretic Text for the scriptural ancestral lineage that separates the two. Contrary to many past chronologists, we pay no attention to the extremely swollen life expectancies for the scriptural patriarchs. If all else is the same, we offer an conceivable family tree beginning with Moses up to Noah dependent on human life expectations. If we take 1460 BC which was the birth date for Abraham and his family, as well as 1660 BC as well as the birth date for Noah and then partitioning by the median number of ages and arriving to the conclusion that the average age was 20 years between Noah or Abraham. This implies that the scriptural patriarchs generally had their children around an average age for the period in the period they lived. This passage doesn't ask us to extend their lives to an unreasonable length.

Illustration 28: Abraham meeting Abimelech, the ruler of the

Philistines.

Utilizing a typical generational duration that is 20 years long, we can reach the conclusion that Abraham was born into the world around 1460 BC. This is consistent with the assertion of the Bible that Abraham had to bargain with the Philistines as he entered Palestine. This is an important issue since archeologists today let us know that Philistines weren't a part of Palestine until 1400 BC. The sequence of translations by The Rabbi Jose ben Halafta and Archbishop James Ussher setting Abraham's date at around 2000 BC is, consequently not be a good idea despite increasing archeological evidence in support of the Philistines were not present in Palestine until around 1400 BC. It is impossible to Abraham to have had a meeting with the Philistine Lord Abimelech within Palestine in the year 2000 BC considering the fact that there was no Philistines existed at the time. This is how we can conclude that the sequence presented here is not just a more comprehensive list of plausible human time intervals for the patriarchs in the scriptural tradition but is also more consistent with the findings of recent research into the prehistoric period in the Holy Land.

In relation to the genealogy of Moses it has been made certain that his father Amran was a descendant of Kohath and not being a child of Kohath according to the way it is usually held. It was extremely common among the older Hebrew copyists to not mention the ancestry of ancestors that weren't relevant to the present topic. The Kohathites were among the four clans that were significant to Levites and the other three clans were those of the Gershonites, Merarites, and Aaronites. The purpose of the representation of Moses' ancestry within the Masoretic Text was only to show that he held an affiliation in Levites. Kohathite clan of Levites. It was not intended to give an age-by-age genealogy back to Abraham and Abraham. This more specific information could have been lost by the period that Moses and his progenitors were slaves in Egypt.

Tabular 6 of Abraham's genealogy displaying an average age of 20 years for Abraham as well as Noah. The date of Noah is determined by an radiocarbon date of Thera ejection. Abraham's dating Abraham is obtained from the ejections crafted by Ahmed Osman. Dating of Moses is taken from the work done by the Roman historian Tacitus. Exertion isn't intended to swell expectations of life expectancy in the Bible to unimaginable lengths.

Noah was born in the year.

1660 BC I

Shem was born in.

1640 BC I

(Note Note: The Thera Eruption, which caused the Great Deluge, was radiocarbon dates to 1627-1600 BC to within an 85% certainty stretch. The Bible informs us that Arphaxad Noah's grandchild was born 2 years following the flood. In the remainder of the book it is noted that we will see that the 1600 BC year of the Thera eruption has been proposed for convenience, but it is completely reliable with evidence of the ejection actually occurred sometime around 1622 BC. This could be the time of the introduction to Arphaxad around 1620 BC just two years following the flood.)

I

Rphaxad, the first of its kind, was conceived around. 1620

BC I

Salah is a concept that was created around.

1600 BC I

ber, conceived ca. 1580

BC I

Peleg was born ca.

1560 BC I

Eu, first conceived around. 1540

BC I

Serug, conceived ca.

1520 BC I

Ahor, who was born ca. 1500

BC I

Erah, born ca.

1480 BC I

braham, who was born around. 1460

BC

(Of noting, Abraham haggled with the Philistines on his arrival within the Holy Land. The Book of Genesis, Abraham signs an "contract in due consideration" to the Philistine leader Abimelech and his family. The Philistines weren't present in Palestine until around. 1400 BC according to the archeological evidence currently in use. In the end, Abraham couldn't have been born in the year 2000 BC which is the standard date given to Abraham by Seder Olam.)

I

saac, conceived ca.

1440 BC I

Acob, born in ca. 1420

BC

(Note The historian Ahmed Osman shows that Jacob's second child Joseph was born into the world in 1400 BC and later became the Grand Vizier in Egypt under the Pharaoh Amenophis III. He is closely related to his Grand Vizier Yuya or Yusef who is famous in Egyptology. Joseph's daughter Tiye got married to Amenophis

III, and became the mom of Akhenaten who was the ancestor of Egyptian monotheism.)

Evi, first conceived in.

1400 BC I

Kohath was created ca.

1380 BC I

Intervening parentage lost

I

Mran, born ca. 820

BC I

Oses, born in the year. 800 BC.

Note that according to Tacitus, Moses drove the Exodus under Pharaoh Bocchoris in the year 720 BC aged the age of 80. The dating of Moses to the time of this date also confirms in a definitive manner that Moses did in fact write his Pentateuch himself, since it is believed that the Old Testament dates to around 700 BC (the hour in the life of Moses.) This evidence-based scriptural sequence changes many centuries in Jewish history.

Abraham was believed to be a scion of around 2000 BC and Moses is believed to date to 1500 BC. However, despite the obvious, the available archaeological and narrative evidence tends to contradict this view. The Jewish faith is considerably older than what has been recently discovered. While the dates listed above may be off by quite a long time, the above sequence, based on an excerpt of hard evidence, is correct +/- 50 years for Noah,

Abraham as well as Moses.

The ancestries presented here are straight out of Exodus Book of Exodus, they are further confirmed by the Jewish-Roman scholar of the history Flavius Josephus. Josephus wrote down the family's history in his work Antiquities of the Jews. There are two sources to prove the family's genealogy: one that is strict and the other secular.

Two sources from different social circles is important. In past times the strict sources, for instance, sanctuary ministers could be a source.

motive to destroy an ancestry record or other verifiable evidence in order to prove a point. For instance, if the prescience of a particular prescience demanded an ancestor's history of that of the Davidic genealogy, that could be a reason for the strict recorders to make lines of descent that mirror the ideal family heritage. For instance, with a Josephus being the case, whatever be it's helpful to study the exact archaeological, common and archeological sources prior to drawing conclusions.

The dating of Moses to around 800 BC is a problem in the conventional account. How do we know that Moses could have come into the world at the age of 800 BC in the event that standard scholars of the past be aware that the House of David started out in the United Kingdom of Israel around 1000 BC? If we accept that Moses was introduced to the world around 800 BC should not each of the Israelites were still in Egypt by the year 1000 BC? The author is of the opinion that at that time a handful of Hebrews who were living in Israel at the time in the Exodus who were evicted through the day of Abraham. Similar to how certain Jews resided at home in Israel throughout their Babylonian bondage, some Jews resided in Israel throughout the Egyptian time period. It's highly unlikely that every Hebrew in the world was sent to Egypt to escape the apex of hunger. There was a chance that a few could have remained in Israel. Perhaps the Hebrew populace at that time had exceeded the limit of conveying agricultural land in Israel. Thus, they needed to separate from the rest of Israel while others migrated to Egypt and where food was plentiful because of the exceptional ripeness that was Egypt's Nile delta.

Conclusion

There is a high probability or even a chance that the hunt for Atlantis will continue to be a long-lasting one. There are many "Atlantists" in the present who are a part of Ignatius Donnelly's excitement for it and have the patience and funds to devote themselves to research , and even undertake adventurous expeditions to the most remote destinations in pursuit of their love. The notion of Atlantis could be an example to"the "perfect society" is a belief held by only a handful of people, probably because of its lack of romance, but there are theories within the more occult and esoteric circles that offer an analogous interpretation to the tale, even if not identical to what Plato believed. William Blake, for example was a believer in Atlantis as an "real" space that was located on a different plane of esoteric realities.

There's a real historical argument in favor of Atlantis that is not often mentioned, yet remains valid as an analogy, or at the very minimum at a "nod" to actual historical actual events. The argument is that Athens is a "perfect society" however, it is at a more recent date Plato as his works suggest. It was the Persian Wars, which involved the vast, culturally rich and sophisticated empire against which Athens even though it was highly exalted in Plato's narrative -and fought. For instance, consider one of the passages from Timaeus's work: "And then it was, Solon, that the menhood of your state made its valour and power in the eyes of the entire world. Because it was the highest of any other gallantry or combative arts, acting in part as the leader of the Greeks as well as being on its own, left out by the rest After enduring the most deadly threats, it defeated invaders, and was awarded a prize and was able to save the people who weren't yet enslaved as well as all of us living within the confines of Heracles the state that it freed without a grudge. [49]

The most memorable moment for Athens in the war with the Persian Empire was it was the Battle of Marathon in 490 BCE. The Athenians recollected this battle as one where they had to defend themselves as the Spartans did not want to fight on the basis that it was on a festival of the Holy Spirit. Then they Athenians came up with an "League" in which they claimed that they were "saved the people from slavery" from the Persians. Perhaps Atlantis was merely the 5th Century Persia with a poetic style? It is possible that this theory can be added to all of the other theories.

In any case, what's interesting concerning the source of Atlantis is that it is the model of excellence, the ideal of culture that was born from an "perfect race" that was never shattered from the grace of God. Based on Plato's narrative of Atlantis its degrading and loss due to The "perfect Athenian society", it is fascinating to find out what he thought of Atlantis its return back to "perfection" with regard to the present mind.

CPSIA information can be obtained
at www.ICGtesting.com
Printed in the USA
BVHW052245090223
658263BV00007B/199